To our Lil ...

Happy Birthday,

all our Luv ...

Taff,

Paul & Kate

xx

DUE SOUTH
Through Tropics and Polar Extremes

First published in hardback in Great Britain in 2009 by:
Wigwam Press Ltd, 204 Latimer Road, London W10 6QY.

Book design by Mary Till
Edited by Richard Madden
Image scanning and retouching by Resolution Creative Ltd - www.resolutioncreative.eu

Printed in China by Imago.

A CIP record for this book is available from the British Library.

ISBN – 978-0-9552192-3-8.

DUE SOUTH
Through Tropics and Polar Extremes

Steve Brooks and Joanna Vestey

Text by Rebecca Stephens
Foreword by Sir Ranulph Fiennes

To Jago and Chloe

FOREWORD

The stories behind great journeys have always captivated me. The great 'firsts' are always compelling, of course, because of the inevitable risks involved and the often life-threatening situations encountered in extreme and darkly beautiful locations. But also because of what they reveal about the personalities involved and the human qualities required to achieve the seemingly impossible.

There are numerous riveting examples. One thinks immediately of Marco Polo travelling fearlessly along the ancient Silk Road and off the map of the known world; or the great Victorian explorers like Speke and Livingstone in the search for the source of the Nile. At the start of the 20th Century, in the shape of men like Shackleton and Scott, the golden age of polar exploration threw up some of the great adventure stories of all time.

But there is also another type of journey that I find equally compelling. Its characteristics are definably British: eccentric, unlikely - both in their conception and their chances of success - and pursued with a dogged single-mindedness that is usually only to be found in a particularly British breed of adventurer.

Steve Brooks and Joanna Vestey fall into both these categories. Not only is their story a first - the first time a single-engine piston helicopter has been flown Pole to Pole - but it is also an absorbing and dramatic story about a couple having the adventure of their lives. Their mad mission? To fly the entire length of the Americas. On their honeymoon!

There is also one other defining characteristic that makes this book so different. Alongside Steve Brooks in the cockpit of their little Robinson 44 helicopter was his co-pilot, Joanna Vestey. As well as being Steve's new bride, Joanna just happened to be an extremely talented photographer whose work for newspapers and magazines around the world and whose many books had already built a formidable reputation.

The result is the story of an extraordinary journey told in words and pictures that captures a unique, and quite literal, cross-section of the world we live in from the frozen Poles to the steaming rainforests of the Amazon and numerous other countries along the way.

With its dramatic and near-fatal ditching in the Drake Passage on the final leg of the journey, it was a story that picked me up and swept me on to what I am relieved to say was a successful and happy conclusion. It will not disappoint!

Sir Ranulph Fiennes

ARCTIC

NORTH AMERICA

CENTRAL AMERICA

SOUTH AMERICA

ANTARCTICA

CONTENTS

INTRODUCTION

There has been many a fine idea hatched over a glass of wine, but few as bold and unimaginably free as that of photographer, Joanna Vestey, and her husband-to-be, Steve Brooks. In the spring of 2002, a date fixed for their wedding in the early summer of the same year, the discussion around the kitchen table at their London home revolved around what they might do for their honeymoon.

The first bat came from Steve. "We could fly the length of the Americas, from Alaska to the southern tip of Chile in a Robinson 44 helicopter." The idea was embraced in a moment. Joanna, like Steve, held a helicopter pilot's licence. They had both been taught by the same man, Quentin Smith, Chief Pilot of HeliAir in Denham. And now Quentin - renowned as a magician in the air and universally known as 'Q' - was included in the conversation as well.

Steve had long wondered whether it might be feasible to fly a single-engine helicopter across the Drake Passage to the Antarctic Peninsula and South Pole - a challenge yet unmet by anybody. Perhaps now was the time for him, with Q, to enter the record books and complete this most southerly leg of the journey?

And the North Pole, what of that? A helicopter had been flown around the world's girth, roughly following the line of the equator, but, as Joanna pointed out, never from top to bottom. And they still had six weeks to go before the wedding.

A plan was agreed. Steve and Q would hop aboard a plane to the U.S. and fly Steve's Robinson 44 G-NUDE - conveniently parked in Alaska - to the North Pole, on the sole condition they would be back in London for the wedding. Steve with Joanna - newly weds on honeymoon - would then return to Alaska and together fly southbound to Chile. There Q would join the expedition once more and attempt a record-breaking flight with Steve across the Drake Passage to the South Pole.

It would be a journey beautiful in its purity of line, from the most northerly point on Earth, through temperate, equatorial and temperate climes again, to the most extreme southerly point on Earth. It would be about 20,000 miles in total in a flying machine comparable in size to the smallest of family cars, sweeping, hovering and lightly touching down on iceberg, beach and forest glade, like a humming bird flitting from flower to flower on a migratory path.

"There's nothing quite like it. They say that to fly is heavenly," says Steve, "but to hover is divine." With a single movement of hand and joystick, pilot and machine levitate into the sky. No runway, no forward speed. It is as if pilot and helicopter are one, flying as one, hovering as one - hanging absolutely stationary in the sky - like an eagle, beady eyes on its prey.

"The helicopter is quite simply the most beautiful thing ever designed," adds Steve. Here speaks the engineer within. Memories from his earliest years are of stripping toy cars to their component parts and reassembling them in an eagerness to understand their workings - an eagerness that led him to read mechanical engineering at university.

But then there is also in Steve, apparent to anyone who shares his company for the briefest moment, a burning desire to pitch personal challenges. "Do we control our destiny, or does destiny control us?" he asks. "Is it simply a matter of belief? If we 'believe' we can achieve something, can we?"

It's no surprise to learn that Steve believes we can achieve pretty much anything to which we set our minds. It is a belief that has served him well in building a property company with his brother, Clive, that is one of the largest shopping centre operators in Northern Europe. He has also succeeded in dedicating decent tracts of time to explorative travel: backpacking through East Africa; kayaking the Zambezi; searching for lost temples in India.

"The real test, though," adds Steve, "is to attempt something that nobody has achieved before. To discover whether something perceived by many as impossible, is in fact possible."

This was one of the driving motives for Steve's quest in March 2001, and again in April 2002, to drive across the Bering Straits - a 56-mile stretch of water, packed solid with ice, that trundles at a steady walking pace ever northwards between the jaws of Russia and the U.S. To attempt this, Steve's creative engineering skills were stretched to the limit. His challenge was to design and pilot an all-terrain amphibious vehicle with the capability of driving through mountains of crushed ice, up and over icebergs and, in the event of a spine-chilling dip in the sea, float and scramble back onto the pack ice.

His solution was eccentric both in concept and to the eye. In essence it was a ski piste basher, with Archimedes screw appendages that doubled up as floats - affectionately known to the team as Snowbird 6. When it came to the test there were some technical problems, inevitably, but the ever-optimistic Steve wasn't deterred. Whenever Snowbird 6 ground to a halt, he'd turn to his co-pilot, Graham Stratford. "Put on your rose-coloured spectacles," he'd say, "we're going outside." And together they'd determinedly find a solution.

His optimism worked - as far as it was permitted. On 7th April 2002, 38 hours after leaving solid American ground, Steve and Graham crossed the international dateline into Russian territory, half way across the Bering Straits. Their intent had been to cross the Bering Straits in its entirety and land victorious on the Russian mainland, but at the eleventh hour the Russians refused them permission.

"It's one of my lasting regrets that we didn't push on regardless," says Steve, "I don't suppose they would have shot us." Nonetheless, it is at least some compensation that in driving across the Bering Straits from the U.S. to Russian territory, Steve and Graham entered the record books as the first people ever to do so. And, as is so often the case, from this adventure flowered another.

"We had Q in a helicopter as support," says Steve. "We'd look up at him, flying unencumbered in the sky. The next adventure, I promised, would be in a helicopter." And so was born Steve's suggestion to Joanna to fly the length of the Americas for their honeymoon and his quest, with Q's help, to be the first to fly a helicopter from Pole to Pole.

Joanna's enthusiasm for their joint flight the length of the Americas was hardly surprising, considering her love of flying and her inherent curiosity about different lands and different peoples manifested in a career in photojournalism. But she was remarkably sanguine about Steve's flight to the North Pole, considering it was to be squeezed into the six weeks immediately prior to their wedding, and to some of the less-than-romantic preparation that would be required for their joint flight so shortly after their wedding. It isn't every bride's dream to spend the first night of her honeymoon in a motel in a Los Angeles suburb across the road from a helicopter factory; but then not every bride is a helicopter pilot.

Flying helicopters had been a natural progression for Joanna. First it was a light aircraft. A friend of her father's flew a Tiger Moth and curiosity led the 21-year-old Joanna to learn to fly as well. Then a career in photojournalism permitted her to follow her lens, always curious, always mindful of the lives of others, moving on from country to country until in August, 1998, her path crossed with Steve's.

Their first helicopter flight together was on Steve's inaugural flight as a qualified pilot; destination, a pleasant country hotel in the Cotswolds for a spot of lunch. Except that they got lost. It was Joanna, peering out of the passenger seat window at a scattering of doubtless perplexed commuters on a railway station platform, who spotted the sign 'Charlbury' and re-established their position on the map.

Though it would be an over-simplification to say that of the two, Steve is the dreamer and Joanna the pragmatist, like all over-simplifications there is in this a grain of truth. It had been Steve's dream, initially, that he and Joanna would fly their little R44 G-NUDE to the North Pole, until Joanna responded matter-of-factly, "Steve, I don't have the experience." Instead, she graciously suggested he might fly with their mutual mentor and instructor, Q, instead.

For Joanna, the challenge - to be the first to fly from a particular Point A to Point B on the map - was of little relevance. Q had opened both Steve's and Joanna's eyes to the joy of what might be called 'helicopter touring', flying off-piste, not from airport to airport but from roof top to back garden, to hideaway beach, to forest glade, to wherever their fancy happened to take them. And with three months to spare, what better way to experience such freedom than on honeymoon in the Americas?

First, though, they had to learn to be safe - which is what brought them to that roadside motel across the road from a helicopter factory. Robinson, manufacturers of R44s, as well as a smaller model, the R22, offers intensive safety-training courses for pilots of its machines at its factory in Torrance, California. Following Steve's North Polar exploits but prior to their odyssey together, Steve and Joanna enrolled for a three-day course.

Day 1. 10th July, 2002, 7.30 a.m. They grab a coffee and a doughnut and take their seats among the 50 or so pilots enrolled for instruction. In turn, the instructor, Tim Tucker, invites them to introduce themselves and briefly outline their experience.

"I'm Todd, I fly lumber in Alaska, I've got 8,000 hours to my name," says the first. "Hi, I'm Chuck, from Texas. I flew Hueys in Vietnam. I've got just 1,500 hours in Robinsons," says another. And so it goes on. The assembly comprises fighter pilots, commercial pilots, ferry pilots - mostly professional, generally with between 500 and 3,000 hours flying experience in Robinson 44s or 22s alone.

Joanna, a little jet-lagged, stands up and explains that she has just flown in from London, that she has 75 hours of flying experience in Robinsons, and that she is about to embark on a 15,000-mile flight from Alaska to Chile. Looks of bewilderment flit around the room. Then Steve stands up and says that he has 120 hours experience, and that he will be flying from Alaska to Chile with Joanna.

Silence prevailed. Here, clearly, were two Brits living up to their well-earned reputation as Great British Amateurs. Yet not a single person in the room could doubt their resolve. Together Joanna and Steve may have accumulated a modest 195 flying hours, but these 195 hours were often in extreme 'off-piste' circumstances with Q, one of the most respected instructors in the business. Their vision was clear and their determination to overcome obstacles absolute. They were eager to learn and, importantly, there was nothing gung-ho about their attitude: safety, in their view, was paramount.

And so they listened and watched with ears and eyes open as Tim Tucker took them through one gruesome home-spun video and then another, each revealing potentially disastrous things that could go wrong. Engine failure, it seems, is the least of one's concerns; a skilled pair of hands can still bring a helicopter down to land. Of real concern is the danger of wire-strikes, flying in bad weather and flying at night. 'Got-to-get-there-itus', the impulse to keep flying, even in deteriorating weather or light conditions, can also be a killer for pilots of helicopters and light aircraft alike.

A mix of these ingredients was probably part of the reason for a number of tragic deaths including that of the legendary racing driver, Graham Hill, who crashed in fog in 1975 and John Kennedy, son of JFK, flying across Atlantic waters to Martha's Vineyard at night in 1999.

Steve and Joanna solemnly set their own rules for their forthcoming trip: no flying in bad weather, no night flying, only limited flying at low levels where cables may be in abundance, and absolutely no arguing in the cockpit.

Easy words to say. Only time would tell how easy they would be to put into practice when the pressure was on.

ARCTIC

All dreams begin somewhere. And for Steve Brooks, that somewhere was the Arctic. With his friend, the legendary pilot Q Smith, their aim was to be the first to fly a single-engine piston helicopter to the North Pole across more than 400 miles of frozen ocean. And this was just the beginning.

NORTH POLE

"The North Pole is like a crown of ice on top of the world. It's also a massive playground - no rules, no laws, no restrictions. The most untamed place on the planet."

Challenges don't come much greater than flying a single-engine helicopter to the North Pole. Ward Hunt Island, from where Steve and Q were to begin their journey, is a bleak, desolate, stretch of snow-covered permafrost on the northernmost tip of Ellesmere Island.

It is here, at 83° 05°N 75°W, that the majority of expeditions to the North Pole depart, the last piece of terra firma before the Pole.

But the challenge was to turn out far greater than even they had expected. At Ward Hunt, Steve and Q were 415 nautical miles from the Pole - a round trip there and back of 830 nautical miles. And yet their helicopter could carry only enough fuel for a range of 600 nautical miles.

A barrel of fuel would have to be dropped off and then relocated later on a moving ice-cap inhabited by hungry polar bears.

But it is the experience itself rather that the scale of the challenge that Steve remembers most. "There are no flags to mark the most northerly point of Earth, no polar research station, and no people. And the beauty of a helicopter is that you can spot land on the Pole."

Flight Information

| FLIGHT DISTANCE | 1,821NM |
| FLIGHT TIME | 15HRS 46MINS |

NORTH POLE:N90° 00.00' E-W00° 00.00'. EXIT:N67° 26.94' W140° 58.22'.

6

HOURS
15h 46m
Arctic

TOTAL HOURS FLOWN
OVER THE ARCTIC

AVERAGE DIRECTION FLOWN
OVER THE ARCTIC

HIGHEST ALTITUDE FLOWN
OVER THE ARCTIC

N

⬡ ARCTIC

North Pole

P1 Fuel

Ward Hunt Island

Eureka

Resolute

ARCTIC
OCEAN

North West Passage Camp

Population: Approx. 4 million
Area: Undefined
Capital City: None
Highest Point: Sea Level at 0m (0ft)
Lowest Point: Fram Basin at -4,665m (-15,304ft)

Sachs Harbour

Zubko

Yukon Camp   Old Crow

BAFFIN
SEA

9%

Journey Length

Cumulative Distance: 1,821nm
Cumulative Time: 15hrs 46mins

-5°

AVERAGE AIR
TEMPERATURE

Month One M T W T F S S M T W T F S S M T W T F S S M T W T F S S M T W T F S S

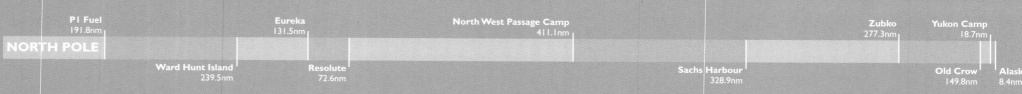

	P1 Fuel 191.8nm		Eureka 131.5nm		North West Passage Camp 411.1nm				Zubko 277.3nm	Yukon Camp 18.7nm
NORTH POLE										
	Ward Hunt Island 239.5nm	Resolute 72.6nm					Sachs Harbour 328.9nm		Old Crow 149.8nm	Alaska 8.4nm

he adventure conceived and with the wedding day fast approaching, there was no time to lose. The six weeks that remained was only just enough time for Steve and Q to fly to the North Pole. So, just a couple of months after their venture on the Bering Straits, Steve and Q, together with HeliAir engineers Simon

Gale and Andrew Russell, flew back across the Atlantic. There they were reunited with Steve's Robinson 44 G-NUDE in a car parking lot at Merrill Field, Anchorage.

"The CAA regulations regarding the servicing of helicopters are extraordinarily strict," Steve points out. "A helicopter registered in

the U.K. must be serviced by U.K.-registered engineers, even if the machine was manufactured in the U.S. and happens, like ours, to be parked in the U.S."

"But other than that a flight to the North Pole is virtually unregulated," he says, a grin spreading across his face. "The South Pole is on land

surrounded by an ocean, but the North Pole is at a point in the ocean surrounded by land. No-one owns the North. It's one of the greatest playgrounds on Earth." The two pilots' boyish enthusiasm at the start of their adventure was palpable. "Nothing had gone wrong at this stage," confesses Steve, "and we were supported by the most generous,

adventurous people imaginable." Alaskans, Steve observes, tend to view themselves as living on the last frontier, wild cousins of mainstream Americans. They're aviation mad; as many as one in sixty Alaskans holds a pilots licence. A Lonely Hearts column in a local paper famously read, "Looking for a life-long companion? Must fly own plane. Please send picture of plane."

And like members of the Alpha Romeo club or Ferrari club beeping at one another on the road, the magnificent men and women of the flying machine club respond to one another with affection all around the globe. Dick Armstrong, owner of Ace Hangers where Steve parked his helicopter, but otherwise a stranger to both pilots, immediately threw them the keys to his lakeside house.

Ron Sheardown, a veteran bush
pilot who famously, and disastrously,
planted the wheels of his heavyweight
Antonov biplane in ice-too-thin at
the North Pole, threw them a gift
of another kind: a rifle, just in case,
for shooting bears. "Nothing was
a problem," says Steve.

So, at 10 a.m. on 3rd June, 2002,
with the little R44 G-NUDE
helicopter heavy of load but the
pilots light of heart, they turned
the key to ignite the helicopter's
Lycoming 540 engine for the first
leg of their extraordinary journey.
This would take them from
Anchorage, 3,000 miles north
across Alaska, along the North
West Passage, and out across
the ice cap to the North Pole.

Immersed in the pioneering
spirit of the likes of Armstrong
and Sheardon, Steve and Q
were blissfully unaware of
the measure of concern, even
controversy, of those in the U.K.
helicopter industry back home.
The flight they were undertaking
would stretch any helicopter
to its limit, and theirs was a tiny
R44 G-NUDE, equipped only
with a single piston-engine to
hold it in the sky.

Typically Steve could see only the
upside. Of the R44 G-NUDE, he
says, "Small, yes, but brilliantly simple
in design, it's the VW Beetle of the
helicopter world. Its size is only an
advantage; it affords us the flexibility
to dip in and out and enjoy the land
we're flying across." And this, Steve
and Q were determined to do. Their
journey north from Anchorage took
them through a remote landscape
of forest and the odd ruler-straight
trunk road to a landscape more
remote still, one of tundra, sparsely
scattered firs, moose and caribou.

Their first stop was Manley Hot
Springs, a remote spa at the head
of a 150-mile road north and west
of Fairbanks, where the two pilots
bathed in the springs and indulged
in a midnight feast in the full
brightness of day. This was, after all,
the land of the midnight sun.

Next step was Old Crow Fort, a lodge across the Canadian border, on the shores of the Yukon River. "Good old gold-mining territory," points out Steve, opportunity for the two adventurers to lower the skids of G-NUDE into the shallow waters of a creek and try their hand at a spot of gold panning. Here they indulged in a spot of fishing too which was about as successful as the panning for gold, before Steve and Q were forced to focus on the task ahead.

Their route led them along a scattering of settlements familiar to few but an elite band of polar travellers whose ambition it is to reach the North Pole: the first, Resolute, a quiet little hamlet of a couple of hundred inhabitants, mostly Inuit, spread along the shore of a permanently frozen lake on Cornwallis Island; then Eureka, a research base on Ellesmere Island; and finally Ward Hunt Island, a bleak, desolate stretch of snow-covered permafrost on the northernmost tip of Ellesmere Island, and the last piece of terra firma before the Pole.

It is here, at 83° 05°N 75°W, that the majority of expeditions to the North Pole depart, and scattered across the snow and ice is a collection of semi-hemispherical huts, like a museum to polar exploration. Steve walked into one. "It was as if someone had just walked out of the door," he says, "there were loaves of bread, quite fresh, and boxes of Special Arctic Expedition Captain Morgan Rum! It was like the Mary Celeste."

Steve and Q arrived at Ward Hunt in early June. A week or two earlier and they might well have been in the company of a polar traveller of two, returning from a long and exhausting walk across the ice cap. But in June the season was over. Steve and Q were alone. There were no polar explorers, no support planes, and beyond this point, no external means to refuel.

This was a challenge. At Ward Hunt, Steve and Q were 415 nautical miles from the Pole

- a round trip there and back of 830 nautical miles; and yet G-NUDE could carry only enough fuel for a range of 600 nautical miles. Somehow, somewhere, they had to dump a barrel of fuel on the polar ice-cap to be able to refuel a part of the way through the journey. All of a sudden, the seriousness of the task ahead was thrown into focus.

"It was clear our first job was to fly a little over 200 miles out onto the ice cap, drop 50 gallons of Avgas and fly back to Ward Hunt," says Steve. "Then we could refuel, fly back the 200 miles or so to our fuel dump and top up the tank with the 50 gallons, which should give the range to fly the remaining 600 miles or so to the Pole and back to Ward Hunt...just!"

There would be precious little spare fuel to steer a circuitous route in the event of bad weather; in such circumstances they'd be forced to land on the ice, and wait. And, crucially, the whole operation was dependent upon their successfully finding their 50 gallon fuel dump once more - not an easy task when the ice pack is on the move at between 1 and 2mph.

"We had a plan," explains Steve. "A GPS (Global Positioning System), attached to the fuel drum, would intermittently transmit its location which we could pick up via a satellite phone to a laptop." In the event, however, sub-zero temperatures resulted in the failure of the GPS transmitter function, and Plan B was the one implemented.

This involved Steve, GPS in hand - operational but for the transmitter - remaining on the ice along with the fuel drum and a radio which only had a limited reception of about 15 miles radius. In the meantime, Q would fly back to Ward Hunt to refuel before being guided back to the fuel dump by Steve on the radio. Weather permitting!

"I had a tent, three or four days' food supply, Ron's rifle, and a

"My mind started playing tricks," remembers Steve. "Blocks of ice were constantly metamorphosing into polar bears."

fishing rod," Steve explains with a smile. "There was nothing out there, not even an aeroplane overhead. I felt completely in awe of the vastness and openness of the place. It's stunning, extraordinarily serene; but yes, my mind definitely started playing tricks. Blocks of ice were constantly metamorphosing into polar bears."

Steve might have expected Q's round trip to take around four hours - five hours maximum. It was eight hours later that Steve's cool nerve was finally rewarded with the reassuring sound of G-NUDE's rotating blades. "Q's an unrushed sort of character," Steve observes.

The tanks filled, they lifted G-NUDE off the ice and flew direction north, the two of them taking turns at the controls. "Sitting in the cockpit, the world opens up before you as if on a TV screen," says Steve. "One moment you're flying over the ocean, then forest, then tundra, and then this vast expanse of ice. We swept low, the skids almost brushing the ice. There were no worries about buildings or wires - it was ultimate freedom. And then there was the icing on the cake: polar bears. I could never have imagined they could be so majestic."

It was 8th June, 2002. Just a couple of hours flying and Steve and Q were fast approaching the North Pole. "The beauty of a helicopter is that you can land spot on the Pole," says Steve - though still it requires delicate manoeuvring. "It's a risky business," he says, "a question of slowly, slowly lowering the skids, bouncing the machine a bit, checking the ice will hold its weight. You don't want to get it wrong."

The two men landed the helicopter within a few metres of the Pole; but Steve wasn't satisfied with this. GPS in hand, he jumped out of the helicopter and ran zig-zagging across the ice, until, "Eeerhaaaar!!!" the GPS read 90.0000 exactly! A quick hop of the helicopter to this precise spot and Steve and Q were perfectly positioned on the very top of the world, an achievement

they celebrated by running in circles round and round the helicopter and - as Steve points out - the world. Nothing seemed more natural than cracking open a bottle of Verve Cliquot - especially as they were surrounded by the world's largest ice bucket.

That night - if you can call it night when the sun is circling above the horizon - Steve and Q pitched camp and rested eight hours or so, listening, senses alert, to the ocean waters lapping the thin skin of ice beneath their heads, and to the odd ominous crack. "There are no flags to mark the most northerly point of Earth, no polar research station, and no people," says Steve. "The ice is always on the move - it arrives one day and is gone the next. There's no sense of history to the place."

To the visual eye, perhaps not; and yet this place, defined only by compass bearing and GPS, is loaded heavily with history, from Robert Peary's disputed claim to have been the first to reach it, in 1909, to the first undisputed sighting of the Pole by Norwegian explorer, Roald Amundsen, and American, Lincoln Ellsworth, from the airship, Norge, on 12th May, 1926. The first undisputed surface journey to the Pole was made by Ralph Plaisted, on a snowmobile, in 1968. A year on, Britain's Wally Herbert became the first to reach the North Pole travelling on foot and by dogsled on the 60th anniversary of Peary's famous, but disputed, expedition.

And then there were the sailors and aviators. The U.S. Navy's Nautilus, the world's first nuclear submarine, passed under the North Pole in 1958; and in 1977 the Soviet Union's Arktika, a nuclear-powered icebreaker, became the first surface ship to navigate the Arctic ice to the North Pole. There is some debate over whether Commander Richard Byrd and co-pilot Floyd Bennett actually managed to fly over the Pole in their Fokker trimotor three days before Amundsen's flight in his dirigible airship; but little argument that U.S. Air Force Lieutenant Colonel Joseph Fletcher and

Lieutenant William Benedict landed a plane at the Pole on 3rd May, 1952.

Many light aircraft - and a few helicopters - have landed at the Pole since, often with the task of picking up travellers who have pitched their stamina and resolve in reaching this most northerly point on Earth by foot. But this was a first for Steve and Q; and more importantly for Steve, this most northerly point on Earth was the starting block for his journey south from the very top of the world to the very bottom of the world. If successful, he would be the first person in the world to fly from the North to the South Pole.

It is ironic that before Steve and Q had even started the engine of G-NUDE for the first leg of this monumental journey, it was the most technologically advanced form of navigation that let them down. A GPS, it seems, fails to function when its dial reads 90.0000N. Indeed, at a point on Earth where every direction is south, which south exactly is the one you want?

Only Q's 24-hour watch face could provide the answer. Pointing the hour hand at the sun, midnight on the watch face marked the Greenwich Meridian. New York, five hours ahead, was at 5 o'clock; Los Angeles, nine hours ahead, was at 9 o'clock; and so on. Resolute, they reckoned, was on the same meridian as New York. So on 9th June, with the hour hand pointing at the sun, Steve and Q set off from the North Pole in the direction of 5 o'clock on Q's watch face, towards Resolute via Ward Hunt and Eureka scooping up their empty fuel drums en route.

Finally they flew back along the North West Passage and across the Yukon and Alaska to Merrill Field in Anchorage, all in good time for a BA trans-Atlantic flight to London for Joanna's and Steve's wedding.

"The GPS read 90 degrees exactly. Steve and Q were perfectly positioned on the very top of the world. They celebrated by running in circles around the helicopter - and indeed the world - before cracking a chilled bottle of Verve Cliquot."

A SHORT HISTORY OF ARCTIC EXPLORATION

The North Pole. The point at the very top of the world at which all lines of longitude converge; where every direction points south; where the Earth's axis of rotation meets the Earth's surface; a point in the middle of the constantly shifting ice of the Arctic Ocean that has drawn pioneering pilots of balloon, fixed wing and rotor aircraft, siren-like, for more than a century.

As early as 1897, Swedish engineer Salamon Andree attempted to fly to the North Pole in a hydrogen-filled balloon, but crashed. He and his two companions were forced to trek across the ice pack to the nearest outcrop of land. Their bodies and diaries revealing their tragic tale were discovered 30 years on. The challenges these men faced over 100 years ago are the same challenges as pilots face today: flat light, blizzards, sub-zero temperatures, head winds, and the practical difficulties of navigation and refuelling (or hydrogen generation).

Although Q Smith, one of the pilots featured in this book, modestly claims that the weather at the Pole can be fine - "like climbing a mountain," he says, "fly north and you can ascend above the cloud" - the truth is that just as on top of a mountain, the weather at the North Pole can also be foul.

An explorer who knew all about extreme polar conditions was the great Norwegian, Roald Amundsen. Best known for pipping Britain's Captain Scott to the South Pole in 1911 and sailing the fabled North West Passage, Amundsen also pioneered the use of aircraft in polar exploration. In 1925, accompanied by the American, Lincoln Ellsworth, Amundsen took two flying boats and headed north landing at 87°44'N - the first landing on the ice anywhere close to the Pole.

The following year, on May 9th, 1926, Commander Richard Byrd with pilot Floyd Bennett claimed to be the first to fly to the North Pole - in a Fokker trimotor. However, though often credited with this most significant of polar firsts, Byrd's account was seriously doubted from the start - particularly among aviators - because of the scant time in which he covered the distance. Byrd claimed to have been aided by helpful tailwinds both there and back, but this wasn't supported by weather reports around the polar rim.

On May 12th, 1926 - just a few days after Byrd's disputed flight to the Pole - Amundsen, together with Ellsworth and the Italian, Umberto Nobile, designer and pilot of the airship Norge, made the first indisputable flight to the North Pole. Sadly, Amundsen died two years later while flying on a rescue mission to find missing members of his friend Nobile's crew whose new airship, Italia, had crashed on the ice.

The outbreak of WWII stemmed pioneering efforts for a while but, discounting Peary's disputed claim of 1909, some sources believe the first men actually to set foot at the North Pole were Soviets. They are variously described as Pavel Gordiyenko and others, or Aleksandr Kuznetsov and others, who landed a plane (or planes) at the North Pole on April 23rd, 1948.

On May 3rd, 1952, U.S. Air Force Lieutenant Colonel Joseph O. Fletcher and Lieutenant William P. Benedict also landed a plane at the North Pole, and some consider this, rather than the Soviet mission, to be the first landing at the Pole. More certainty surrounds the first helicopter flight. This was piloted by Australian adventurer and philanthropist, Dick Smith, who successfully flew to the Pole in 1987 in a Bell 206B Jetranger III while Steve Brooks' and Q Smith's flight was the first in a piston-powered helicopter.

"Best known for pipping Britain's Captain Scott to the South Pole in 1911, Roald Amundsen also pioneered the use of aircraft in polar exploration."

NORTH AMERICA

Criss-crossing America, whether it be by car, Greyhound, or pogo stick was made famous by the Beat generation and remains one of the most iconic of journeys. How much more so on your honeymoon in a Robinson 44 helicopter. Steve's and Joanna's flight together was about to begin.

ALASKA

*"Alaska is America's final frontier.
It's where everyone goes to escape
from the norm. To both find themselves
and lose themselves."*

The first three days of Steve's and Joanna's honeymoon had been spent at the Robinson helicopter factory in Torrance, California, on an intensive safety-training course. To date Steve had just 120 hours flying Robinson 44s under his belt - including his journey to the North Pole with Q - while Joanna had just 72 hours.

Ahead of them lay a 15,000-mile journey from Alaska down the length of the Americas to Punta Arenas at the southern tip of Chile. Their flying machine was comparable in size to the smallest of family cars but also capable of sweeping, hovering and lightly touching down on iceberg, beach and forest glade. Like a humming bird, in fact, flitting from flower to flower on a migratory path.

The inaugural leg of their journey was from Merrill Field in Anchorage to the state capital of Juneau, 500 miles to the south east. "Our first flight was magical," Joanna recalls. "We flew over forests and glaciers spotting bears and moose and at one point some eagles took a dive at our rotors."

Flight Information

| FLIGHT DISTANCE | 1,208NM |
| FLIGHT TIME | 10HRS 28MINS |

ENTRY: N67° 26.94′ W140° 58.22′.   EXIT: N54° 42.40′ W130° 49.37′.

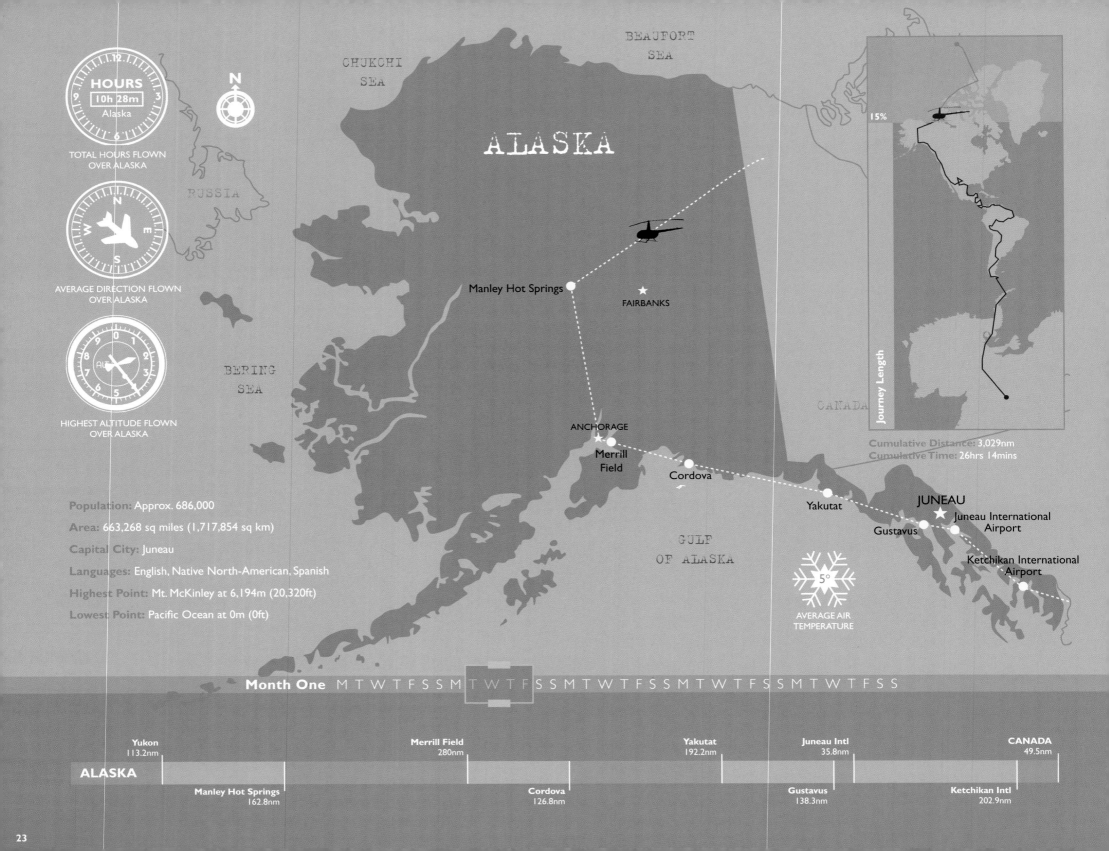

HOURS
10h 28m
Alaska
TOTAL HOURS FLOWN
OVER ALASKA

N

AVERAGE DIRECTION FLOWN
OVER ALASKA

HIGHEST ALTITUDE FLOWN
OVER ALASKA

CHUKCHI
SEA

BEAUFORT
SEA

ALASKA

RUSSIA

BERING
SEA

Manley Hot Springs

FAIRBANKS

15%

Journey Length

CANADA

Cumulative Distance: 3,029nm
Cumulative Time: 26hrs 14mins

ANCHORAGE

Merrill
Field

Cordova

Yakutat

JUNEAU

Juneau International
Airport

Gustavus

Ketchikan International
Airport

Population: Approx. 686,000

Area: 663,268 sq miles (1,717,854 sq km)

Capital City: Juneau

Languages: English, Native North-American, Spanish

Highest Point: Mt. McKinley at 6,194m (20,320ft)

Lowest Point: Pacific Ocean at 0m (0ft)

GULF
OF ALASKA

5°

AVERAGE AIR
TEMPERATURE

Month One M T W T F S S M T W T F S S M T W T F S S M T W T F S S

Yukon
113.2nm

Merrill Field
280nm

Yakutat
192.2nm

Juneau Intl
35.8nm

CANADA
49.5nm

ALASKA

Manley Hot Springs
162.8nm

Cordova
126.8nm

Gustavus
138.3nm

Ketchikan Intl
202.9nm

23

A flight to the North Pole, a wedding and a Robinson's safety-training course completed, next on Steve's and Joanna's list was to ensure that the R44 G-NUDE was in good flying order for the long journey ahead. They flew from Los Angeles to Anchorage to meet British engineers, Andy and Simon, who had flown

across the Atlantic once again to service the helicopter at Merrill Field.

Dick Armstrong was there, throwing them the keys to his car and offering unconditional hospitality. A short 13-minute flight and they were in his waterside cabin on Big Lake, where he generously imparted all he knew about American air space

regulations - quite different, as it turned out, from British regulations - as were radiotelephony procedures, navigation systems, maps and charts. Only the use of the English language was thankfully familiar, together with the universal use of imperial feet as the measure of altitude.

Steve and Joanna had put much into the planning of this longest leg

of the trip over the previous few months. Both had learnt to fly in Robinson 22s, a small, two-seater helicopter. Theirs was a four-seater Robinson 44 and they'd had to train for a new license to fly it. Joanna, a feather-light 5'2" laughed when she relayed that she'd been obliged to throw a 'bucket of lead' under her seat to balance the weight of this larger aircraft.

It was Steve the mechanical engineer's job to put together an emergency tool kit and a few essential spare parts. Flying from one end of the Americas to the other, they'd require different fuel filters for different fuels and different oils for different temperatures.

There would be different languages to contend with as well. Joanna

jumped at the opportunity to spend a couple of weeks in Spain, taking a crash course in Spanish to at least cover her in large chunks of Central and South America.

And then there was the big question: what route exactly were they to take? Both were familiar with North America, but pretty vague when it came to Central

24

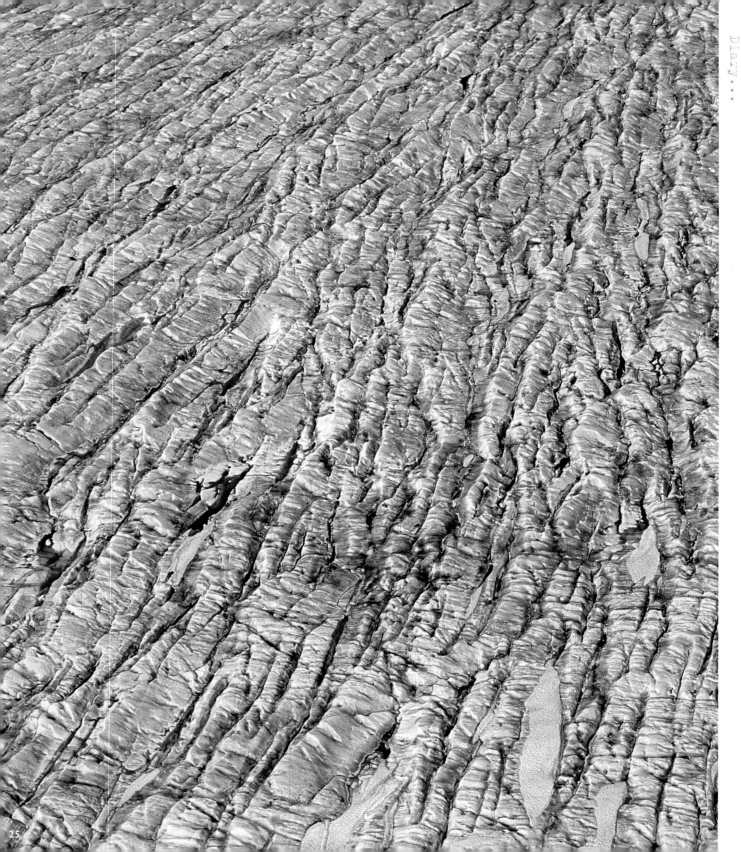

and South America. That was the joy, to explore new lands. And though they both would have loved to have left room for as much flexibility as possible, to discover and explore as they ventured further south, there was by necessity a degree of route mapping to be done. Unlike a backpacker (though in spirit that is exactly what they were), they had to consider that the maximum range of their helicopter was around 400 miles. So where could they refuel? Where were the airfields? And where and when were they to cross borders from one state to another and one country to another?

There was much searching of the Internet and noses buried in Lonely Planet guide books to ensure that they made the best possible choices on what would be, quite literally, a once in a life time odyssey. They wanted to pick the plums, but then they had to be practical too. They had long conversations with a aviation company called Overflight in the U.K., who would arrange flight clearances, landing permits, traffic rights and flight plans for the entire length of their trip from Anchorage through to Punta Arenas.

And finally they had to get themselves and engineers Andy and Simon to the United States. In many ways the planning and preparation had felt like an expedition in itself. Unbelievably, all that was left to do now was to hop back from Dick Armstong's cabin to Ace Hangers and pack. Again, not a task to be undertaken without careful thought. A R44 G-NUDE weighs in at 1,500lbs; and its maximum total flying weight is 2,400lbs, much of which is fuel.

There was a great deal of busy packing, and then unpacking. Suitcases of superfluous items flown from one side of the Atlantic to the other were handed to Simon and Andrew to carry back again. Meanwhile Joanna and Steve puzzled over the essential items to bring: survival gear, camping kit, cooking equipment, camera bag, batteries, water, dried food, a can of bear spray. All these left just a few cubic inches to slot in a small overnight bag with a change of clothes.

Finally, they were ready to embark on the first leg of their epic 15,000-mile journey from Anchorage, Alaska, to the frontier town of Punta Arenas at the very southern tip of Chile.

"We flew over forests and glaciers spotting bears and moose and at one point, flying low over turquoise glacial melt water, watched with amazement as eagles took a dive at our rotors."

It was 16th July, 2002. First stop, the state capital city of Juneau, some 500 miles to the south east. "Our first flight of the journey was magical," Joanna recalls, "up through hills and sweeping valleys, patches of snow atop and waterfalls cascading into rivers. We flew over forests and glaciers spotting bears and moose, and at one point, flying low over opaque, turquoise glacial melt-water, watched with amazement as eagles took a dive at our rotors."

A single stop to refuel at Cordova, a small town near the mouth of the Copper River, might have afforded them sufficient range to Juneau. Except that a disturbingly fast swing of the fuel gauge enforced a landing at Gustavus, a tiny town some 36 nautical miles short, where they discovered to mixed amusement and dismay that they had left the fuel cap behind at Cordova!

Easily fixed - a spare one was at hand - and soon they were on their onward journey over the Lynn Canal to the international airport at Juneau. Curiously Juneau, a long time favoured fishing area for the local Tlingit people and named, in 1881, after gold prospector Joe Juneau, is the only mainland state capital in the U.S. which has no roads leading to it. It is only accessible via sea or air.

"It's one of my lasting impressions of the trip," says Steve, in words comforting to those of us concerned about the overpopulation of our planet, "that much that we flew over was wilderness - mile upon mile upon mile of forest, mountain and desert - before occasionally dipping into really very small, heavily populated, urbanisations."

Juneau is one such urbanisation. Downtown, at sea level, it is a cultural centre for the Tlingit, Haida and Tsimshian people of south east Alaska, a town also steeped in gold mining history and a major destination for around a million tourists who arrive by cruise ship every year. But around this hive of human activity, nature pushes in on all sides.

The town is surrounded by steep mountains, 3,500 - 4,000ft high, capped with a vast ice cap from which some 30 glaciers flow into valley and sea. One of these, visible from the local road system, is the Mendenhall. And in view of this, tucked away in a tranquil forest, Joanna and Steve enjoyed the luxury of resting for a couple of days in a small, boutique hotel, planning future legs of the flight and finally catching breath after the social and administrative whirlwind of the previous weeks.

"A lonely hearts column in a local paper famously reads: "Looking for a life-long companion? Must fly own plane. Please send picture of plane."

ALASKA - LAND OF THE PRIVATE PLANE

"Take a 10-minute flight or walk for a week." A banner stretched across the street of a one-horse town in upstate Alaska lures travellers into Alaska's wild, unspoiled land of bears, bald eagles and solitude. The fact is that Alaska is so vast, the land so boggy or else so mountainous, and roads so scarce, that often the only practical means of travel is by air.

It isn't surprising then, that a substantial number of inhabitants have both a private pilot licence and their own plane. For the luxury homes surrounding Anchorage's Campbell Lake, a brace of cars in the garage and a Cessna 185 tied to the dock is the norm; and a couple of miles north, Lake Hood is the world's most active seaplane base.

Alaska has about 8,000 registered aircraft and almost 11,000 licensed pilots among its 686,000 residents. That is six times as many pilots and 16 times as many aircraft per capita as the rest of the U.S. combined. Airports and runways are dotted about the state but, by necessity, pilots in Alaska fit their planes with fat tundra tyres, skis or floats to enable them to land on beaches, snowfields and lakes. Often the only landing spot is where the pilot makes one, and although this carries with it enormous freedom, it also carries risk.

Many pilots cautiously limit their flying to the long, warm days of the summer months; but for those who brave flying around the time of the winter solstice, flying conditions in such a northerly, remote and rugged country are a very serious matter. White-outs, high winds, sub-zero temperatures and poor visibility are to be expected, and accidents are common. The Federal Aviation Administration records there were 84 general accidents in Alaska in 2008 in which 14 people were killed, and that this is not unusual.

Top of any pilot's list of considerations is Alaska's harsh and unpredictable weather. Satellite forecasting and live weather cams offer information that could only have been dreamt of a decade ago, but still a seasoned pilot seeks advice from real human beings with up-to-the-minute information on conditions over a particular pass, or at a particular landing strip; and still he or she flies prepared for the worst.

Mechanical problems or a turn in the weather can all too often force an unscheduled landing until conditions improve, and then survival gear is essential - that, and a satellite phone to communicate all is well. Too many people have been killed on search and rescue missions to save others, so it's best not to get into trouble in the first place, if at all possible. They have a saying in Alaska: "See you tomorrow, weather permitting."

"The fact is that Alaska is so vast, the land so boggy or else so mountainous, and roads so scarce, that often the only practical means of travel is by air."

CANADA

"Planet Earth started to come to life again. With the frozen seas behind us, this was a land where you could fish, hunt, pick flowers and eat strawberries."

With the frozen wastes of Alaska and the far north now behind them, Joanna and Steve were beginning to settle into the journey. From Alaska, their route took them down the west coast of Canada and out over Queen Charlotte Sound where they could see tiny, densely forested islands far below them.

It was on this stretch, in an area renowned for its 100 inches of rainfall a year, that they found themselves already breaking rule number one of the safety mantra: no flying in bad weather. But as the light began to fade and the weather deteriorate, it was also their first real taste of the wilderness flying they had dreamt about for so long.

After a flight over a series of off-shore islands with a dearth of landing options, they at last found a slender spit of sand high and dry above the water line. On a remote island with just bear prints in the sand for company, they had finally found the freedom they craved. "It was the realisation of our dream, our moment of arrival," says Steve now.

Flight Information

FLIGHT DISTANCE	547NM
FLIGHT TIME	4HRS 44MINS

ENTRY: N54° 42.40' W130° 49.37'. EXIT: N49° 00.17' W122° 25.74'.

32

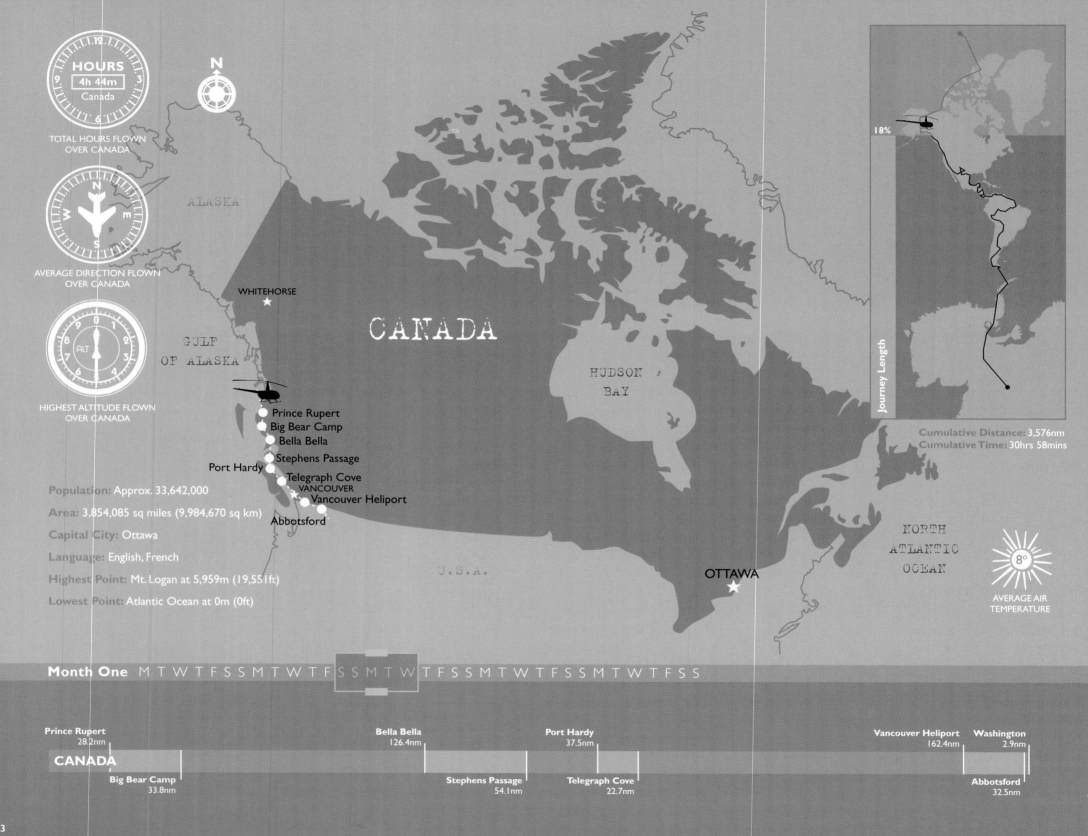

HOURS
4h 44m
Canada

TOTAL HOURS FLOWN
OVER CANADA

N

AVERAGE DIRECTION FLOWN
OVER CANADA

ALT

HIGHEST ALTITUDE FLOWN
OVER CANADA

N

ALASKA

WHITEHORSE

GULF
OF ALASKA

CANADA

HUDSON
BAY

Population: Approx. 33,642,000

Area: 3,854,085 sq miles (9,984,670 sq km)

Capital City: Ottawa

Language: English, French

Highest Point: Mt. Logan at 5,959m (19,551ft)

Lowest Point: Atlantic Ocean at 0m (0ft)

Prince Rupert
Big Bear Camp
Bella Bella
Stephens Passage
Port Hardy
Telegraph Cove
VANCOUVER
Vancouver Heliport
Abbotsford

U.S.A.

OTTAWA

NORTH
ATLANTIC
OCEAN

8°

AVERAGE AIR
TEMPERATURE

18%

Journey Length

Cumulative Distance: 3,576nm
Cumulative Time: 30hrs 58mins

Month One M T W T F S S M T W T F S S M T W T F S S M T W T F S S M T W T F S S

Prince Rupert
28.2nm

CANADA

Big Bear Camp
33.8nm

Bella Bella
126.4nm

Stephens Passage
54.1nm

Port Hardy
37.5nm

Telegraph Cove
22.7nm

Vancouver Heliport
162.4nm

Washington
2.9nm

Abbotsford
32.5nm

heir next step was Prince Rupert, just over the Canadian border. En route they couldn't resist the allure of a remote beach with, in Joanna's words, "some spectacularly good bergy bits on it" - large pieces of ancient glacial ice that had been carried down the sound and washed up with the tide.

The photographer in Joanna came to the fore and they landed G-NUDE to capture images of these exquisite, ethereal formations, creaking and snapping, slowly dripping into the sands.

Due to the delay, they arrived a little late to clear customs at Prince Rupert and flying on,

direction south, towards Vancouver over open water and tiny, densely forested islands, the light began to fade and the weather deteriorate. An area renowned for its 100 inches of rainfall a year was living up to its reputation; and only a few days into their trip, Joanna and Steve were already breaking rule number one of their safety mantra: no flying in bad weather.

"Flying 600 to 700 miles in a day, you see different weather patterns all the time," says Steve. "It isn't just the landscapes and the people that change, but the temperature, altitude and humidity. We were dipping into the unknown all the time and fully aware of it. In reality," he concludes, "it was impossible not to fly in bad weather."

"There were huge bear foot prints in the soil," says Joanna, "and frankly I didn't know the first thing about survival."

Steve's and Joanna's reality in this moment was that, as well as the light and weather deteriorating, the tide was running high. Slithers of beach that had once beckoned as perfect landing spots had all but disappeared, and all that remained was open sea, or else islands carpeted, water's edge to water's edge, in forest. Where the hell to land?

All senses on full alert, Steve and Joanna flew on, eagle eyes scanning the horizon for a place to land until, at last, they spotted a slender spit of sand between two islands, high and dry above the water line. Slowly they brought the helicopter down and jumped, hugely relieved, onto firm ground.

It wasn't time yet, though, to put anxiety to bed. "The tide was still rising. We didn't know if it was going to swamp the helicopter. There were huge bear footprints in the soil," says Joanna, "and frankly I didn't know the first thing about survival." But importantly - and both Joanna and Steve felt this in equal measure - they had escaped the system. Though never truly isolated from civilization as long as there is a satellite telephone at hand, they had nonetheless found themselves on an island with no roads, no telegraph poles, and no people. "It was the realisation of our dream, our moment of arrival," says Steve.

Together they pitched camp and foraged around for some sodden firewood and with the help of a little Avgas siphoned from the helicopter fuel tank, lit a fire. Joanna is a good shopper and a good cook: before leaving Prince Rupert she had picked up a couple of steaks, some vegetables, and a decent red wine; and now she prepared them, al fresco, while Steve strummed his travel guitar in the drizzle.

The following morning brought only more rain. Steve's rose-tinted glasses had him lift G-NUDE 20ft off the ground before common sense prevailed and he landed her again, in exactly the same spot that he had taken off. There was little to

be done but fish (a copper bottom rock fish for the record), gather mussels...and wait.

In the late afternoon the clouds finally began to part. No time to lose. Joanna and Steve hastily struck camp, undertook the necessary safety checks, and took to the air. The weather was far from perfect but, as Q had taught them, they "flew to what they could see" scraping around the edges of islands and inlets at about 100ft, one-mile visibility and 300ft cloud base.

Their first destination was Port Hardy where they briefly stopped to refuel before heading 20 miles further south to Telegraph Cove on the north east of Vancouver Island. Even here there were few places to land. Eventually they touched down in a car park on the edge of town and wandered into the centre returning a couple of hours later to their first, and only, parking ticket of the expedition stuck on the windscreen of G-NUDE.

Telegraph Cove is a small, picturesque community, which grew out of a one-room station at the northern terminus of the Campbell River Telegraph Line. Today it is primarily a send-off point for kayakers and whale-watchers keen to view the large numbers of orcas that spend the summer months in the nearby Johnstone Strait, separating the northern part of Vancouver Island from mainland British Columbia. Joanna and Steve were on honeymoon; they, too, wished to view the majestic orcas as well as the black bears, which they watched, wide-eyed, scavenging the off-casts from a fish cannery at a local dump.

Their last stop in Canada, before heading over the U.S. border for clearance at Bellingham, was Vancouver. "What a city!" exclaims Steve. "My favourite in the world. It was wonderful to fly in from the back and beyond, over the Strait of Georgia and between the city's towering office blocks, gleaming in the sun, to land at Vancouver Harbour Heliport right in the centre of town."

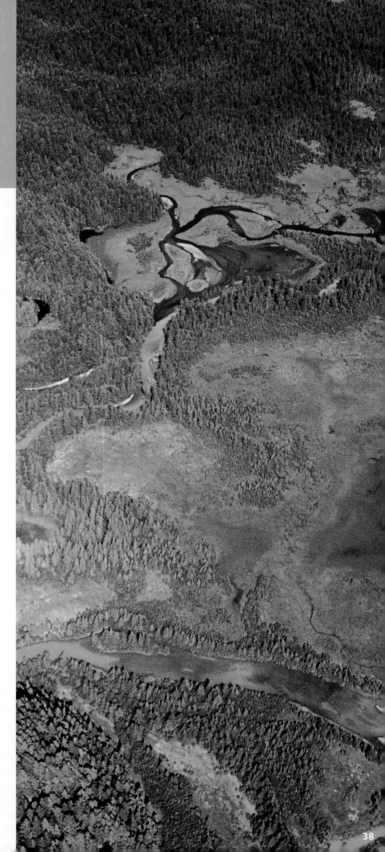

THE KLONDIKE GOLD RUSH

On August 16th, 1896, Californian George Washington Carmack and two Indian friends, Skookum Jim and Tagish Charley, pried a thumb-sized nugget of gold from the bed of Rabbit Creek, a tributary of the Klondike River in Canada's Yukon Territory. It was an action that was to set in motion one of the most frenzied and fabled gold rushes in history.

Heavy snow falls and frozen lines of communication kept the strike a secret from all but local prospectors for almost a year. But the following July, when steamships from Alaska docked in San Francisco and Seattle and a few tens of dishevelled miners disembarked - heavily loaded with boxes and blankets and coffee cans full of gold - Klondike fever took hold and quickly reached epidemic proportions.

'GOLD! GOLD! GOLD! GOLD!' read the headline of the Seattle Post-Intelligencer. The U.S. had been in deep economic depression for 30 years, particularly the Pacific North West; people were tired of being poor, and responded in droves. In Seattle alone, 2,800 eager would-be prospectors packed their bags in a single week; altogether an estimated 100,000 people, mainly from the U.S., set out for the new gold fields with dreams of a quick buck to be made.

But fewer than half that number made it to their destination, and precious few of them made their fortune. The journey to the Klondike was long, arduous and often dangerous. Steamers from Vancouver, Victoria, Seattle and San Francisco, destined for Skagway or its neighbouring town Dyea in the Alaska panhandle, were loaded to full capacity. So paddle wheelers, fishing vessels and barges were added to the fleet, many unseaworthy, all overloaded - 'floating coffins' that frequently lived up to their name.

And then from the tidal flats of Skagway and Dyea, there was the big climb over the Coast Mountains and the U.S./Canada border to Bennet Lake, British Columbia, along the treacherous White Pass Trail (quickly dubbed Dead Horse Trail). Alternatively, there was the painfully steep 1,000ft 'Golden Stairs' of the Chilkoot Trail.

Red-coated North West Mounted Police awaited, to enforce law and order, but also to collect duty and - a new law this - to ensure each prospector entering Canada carried one ton of supplies to ensure survival through the winter, placing a huge burden on prospector and pack animal alike. "Neither law nor order prevailed, honest persons had no protection from the gang of rascals who plied their nefarious trade," wrote mounted police office Sam Steele, describing the scene at the base of the treacherous Chilkoot Pass. "Might was right; murder, robbery, and petty theft were common occurrences."

The last leg of the journey was relatively calm by comparison, a float down the Yukon River to the new gold rush town of Dawson. But for many, their efforts were in vain: most of the paying claims were staked out and filed in the six months after August 16th, 1896. More successful was a smaller, cannier contingent of entrepreneurial men and women who prospered off the back of those with Klondike fever - the outfitters, packers, mule drivers, clairvoyants, and bakers of good old American apple pies.

"Altogether an estimated 100,000 people, mainly from the U.S., set out for the new gold fields with dreams of a quick buck to be made."

"Cloud was virtually seeping through the doors of the helicopter and into our pockets," Joanna recalls. "It was amazing to watch it rolling in from the sea, smothering the land beneath."

WASHINGTON & OREGON

"On one level we were back in civilization again. The forests and the giant redwoods were a joy to fly over. But the fog could be a real nightmare, our biggest fear. It could all have been over in seconds."

From Vancouver Joanna and Steve flew south crossing the border into the U.S. and on to the next stage of their journey. Hugging the coast of first Washington and then Oregon, they were frequently dazzled by stunning forest landscapes but one thought was always in the back of their minds. The weather.

Nothing puts more doubt in a pilot's mind than the inevitable uncertainty in even the most accurate forecast. Ask any pilot: the only fool-proof weather forecast known to man is the one you are looking at out of the cockpit window right now.

And nowhere is this more true than the Pacific coast of the U.S. The coastal climate of both Oregon and Washington is heavily influenced by the Pacific Ocean. This is caused in large part by the damp air mass blowing in off the Pacific Ocean condensing over the heavily-wooded mountain forests and causing a navigational nightmare for Steve and Joanna as they increasingly found themselves blanketed in thick fog.

Flight Information

FLIGHT DISTANCE	375NM
FLIGHT TIME	3HRS 15MINS

ENTRY:N49° 00.17′ W122° 25.74′.   EXIT:N42° 01.36′ W123° 59.10′.

40

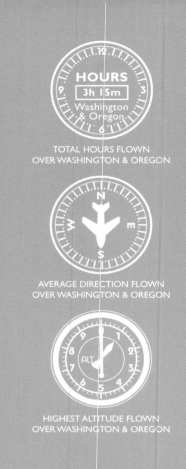

HOURS

3h 15m
Washington & Oregon

TOTAL HOURS FLOWN
OVER WASHINGTON & OREGON

AVERAGE DIRECTION FLOWN
OVER WASHINGTON & OREGON

ALT

HIGHEST ALTITUDE FLOWN
OVER WASHINGTON & OREGON

N

Bellingham International Airport

SEATTLE

WASHINGTON

NORTH
PACIFIC
OCEAN

Astoria

PORTLAND

SALEM

OREGON

North Bend Municipal Airport

Big Surf Camp

10°

AVERAGE AIR
TEMPERATURE

IDAHO

20%

Journey Length

Cumulative Distance: 3,952nm
Cumulative Time: 34hrs 13mins

WASHINGTON

Population: Approx. 6,550,000

Area: 71,342 sq miles (184,827 sq km)

Capital City: Seattle

Language: English

Highest Point: Mt. Rainier
at 4,392 m (14,410ft)

Lowest Point: Pacific Ocean
at 0m (0ft)

OREGON

Population: Approx. 3,790,000

Area: 98,466 sq miles (255,026 sq km)

Capital City: Salem

Language: English

Highest Point: Mt. Hood at 3,426m (11,239ft)

Lowest Point: Pacific Ocean 0m (0ft)

Month One M T W T F S S M T W T F S S M T W T F S S M T W T F S S M T W T F S S

Bellingham Intl
13.3nm

WASHINGTON

Astoria
167.2nm

North Bend Mun
165.2nm

Big Surf Camp
27.2nm

California
62.1nm

The next leg of the journey was through the western states of the U.S. It was a country with which they were both reasonably familiar. Steve, in particular, had spent a considerable amount of time here on business.

Once customs were cleared at Bellingham, Washington State, they flew south to Bandon and then headed on towards Crescent City in Oregon.

"Cloud was virtually seeping through the doors of the helicopter and into our pockets," Joanna explains. "It was amazing to watch it rolling in from the sea, smothering the land beneath."

And alarming, too. Joanna and Steve, their safety training playing real dividends, had been obliged to fly slowly, cautiously, beneath the cloud, as far as it was possible. Now they were heading away from the coast and into the rolling, forest-covered hills where the air was clear and the landscape breathtakingly beautiful.

But then they had to dip back down to the coast again for fuel, once again forced to fly at low level, scraping along a narrow river valley beneath the cloud. "We were particularly aware of the possibility of cables in the valley," says Steve.

"They tend to stretch from one side of the valley to the other, and you can't see them. You just have to keep your eyes peeled for pylons and make sure you have an escape route if anything looms up at you in the mist. That means hugging one or other side of the valley, so you have space to turn sharply to the left or right, and swoop away from trouble."

A touch tense, they finally landed at Crescent City airfield. There were deer grazing the verges of the runway; no-one had been there for days. "The boys at the airfield were pretty amazed to see us," says Steve - unsurprisingly perhaps, considering the coastal highway is usually shrouded in mist for three months of the year until September.

CLOUD OF SUSPICION

On the ground, a spot of cloud might be a minor inconvenience. In the sky, it can be the difference between life and death. Helicopter pilots take the weather extremely seriously indeed.

Simply put, when a helicopter pilot lifts off the ground, he or she has one of two ways of flying: either by Visual Flight Rules (VFR) or Instrument Flight Rules (IFR). All helicopter pilots in the possession of a private pilot licence are qualified to fly by VFR, namely in sight of the ground, clear of cloud, at day or night. Fine weather flying.

In order to be able to fly in poor visibility and through cloud, a pilot must also have instrument rating qualifications. Even if nothing can be seen out of the cockpit window, an IFR-rated pilot can still fly while looking only at the instrument panel and is authorised to fly through cloud using Air Traffic Control procedures designed to maintain separation from other aircraft.

Most commercial flights operate exclusively under IFR, but private, recreational flights - including that of Steve's and Joanna's - often operate under VFR. This is either because the pilots aren't IFR-rated, or because their helicopter has a single-engine - in the UK it is a legal requirement that all IFR helicopters are twin-engine - or simply because they enjoy the freedom.

Under VFR, it is the pilot who assumes responsibility for navigation and separation from other aircraft. The pilot is expected to 'see and avoid' obstacles and generally is not given routes or altitudes by Air Traffic Control. However, he or she is required to have a

transponder to help identify the helicopter on radar near busier airports and while operating in certain types of airspace.

Governing agencies - the Civil Aviation Authority in the UK and Federal Aviation Administration in the U.S. - have established specific 'fine' weather requirements for helicopters flying under VFR. These include minimum visibility and distance from clouds to ensure that the helicopter pilot can see and, of course, be seen by others.

The problem arises when the weather, ever unpredictable, changes during flight, as Joanna and Steve experienced with the cloud rolling off the sea in Oregon. Many helicopter pilots have experienced the tension rising in the cockpit as they have been obliged to fumble along at low level, eyes popping out of their sockets as they scour the ground for tall buildings and power cables in an attempt to find a safe landing. Over water it can be worse, if the cloud base lowers and the pilot is all of a sudden in a goldfish bowl of murk, at very low altitude, unable to distinguish the horizon.

In this situation, the IFR helicopter is able to take the safe way out – up! The VFR helicopter can also go up, but into what? Many accidents are the result of VFR helicopters flying into situations where suddenly the one thing they are totally reliant upon - their horizon - is stolen from them.

There is only one way to stay safe when flying by VFR and that is to stick to the rules: no flying in poor visibility, or through cloud, especially at night. The trouble is that changing circumstances in remote regions with poor meteorological information can on occasions make these rules difficult to observe.

"On the ground, a spot of cloud might be a minor inconvenience. In the sky, it can be the difference between life and death."

CALIFORNIA

"Suddenly everything was hot and dry again and the heat was sometimes intense. But beneath us everything was very orderly with wide open spaces, orange groves and vineyards everywhere."

After the frozen northlands of Alaska followed by the wet and damp of the Pacific north-west, Joanna and Steve were at last approaching more tropical climes. In its more northerly latitudes, California is characterised by the same Redwood and Douglas fir forests they had encountered in Washington and Oregon, home in fact to some of the largest, oldest, and tallest trees in the world.

But further south the landscape opens out into the flat, heavily cultivated Central Valley which extends 400 miles from the lush Sacramento Valley in the north to the dry, semi-arid San Joaquin Valley in the south. With its vineyards and fruit farms, it is one of the most productive agricultural regions on Earth.

This sudden burst of tropical temperatures was a short introduction for the desert landscapes that awaited them as they made their way inland towards Arizona and Texas. As well as being one of the hottest, driest places in the western hemisphere, the Mojave Desert is also home to the Mojave Air and Space Port where the sub-orbital SpaceShipOne was designed and built.

Flight Information

FLIGHT DISTANCE	622NM
FLIGHT TIME	5HRS 23MINS

ENTRY:N42° 01.36' W123° 59.10'.   EXIT:N34° 54.30' W114° 37.68'.

46

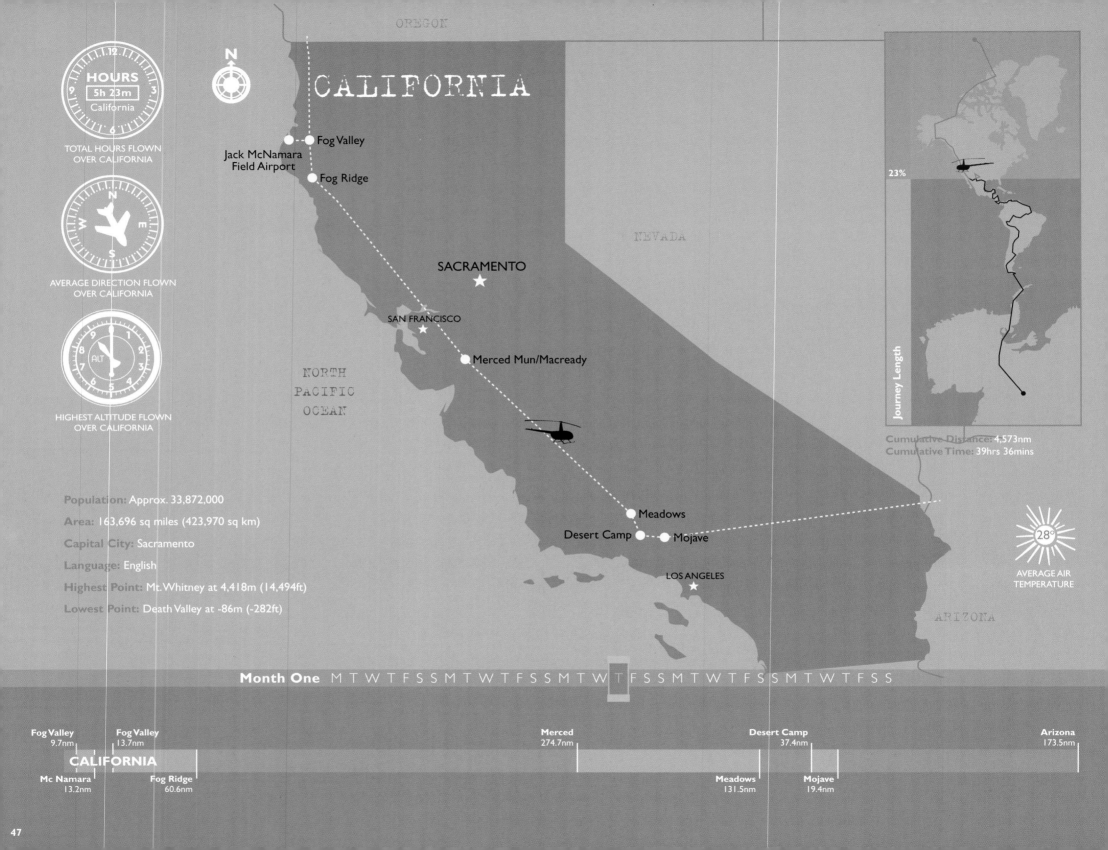

HOURS
5h 23m
California

TOTAL HOURS FLOWN
OVER CALIFORNIA

N

AVERAGE DIRECTION FLOWN
OVER CALIFORNIA

ALT

HIGHEST ALTITUDE FLOWN
OVER CALIFORNIA

Population: Approx. 33,872,000

Area: 163,696 sq miles (423,970 sq km)

Capital City: Sacramento

Language: English

Highest Point: Mt. Whitney at 4,418m (14,494ft)

Lowest Point: Death Valley at -86m (-282ft)

OREGON

CALIFORNIA

Fog Valley

Jack McNamara
Field Airport

Fog Ridge

NEVADA

SACRAMENTO

NORTH
PACIFIC
OCEAN

SAN FRANCISCO

Merced Mun/Macready

Meadows

Desert Camp   Mojave

LOS ANGELES

ARIZONA

23%

Journey Length

Cumulative Distance: 4,573nm
Cumulative Time: 39hrs 36mins

28°

AVERAGE AIR
TEMPERATURE

Month One M T W T F S S M T W T F S S M T W T F S S M T W T F S S M T W T F S S

Fog Valley
9.7nm

Fog Valley
13.7nm

Merced
274.7nm

Desert Camp
37.4nm

Arizona
173.5nm

CALIFORNIA

Mc Namara
13.2nm

Fog Ridge
60.6nm

Meadows
131.5nm

Mojave
19.4nm

47

Diary .

With the dangers of low-lying mist and fog in mind, Joanna and Steve opted to take a south-easterly course away from the ocean and over the Coast Range. "It's just incredible the speed at which the scenery changes," says Joanna. "One minute we were flying through huge passes and over forested hills, and the next across the vast low-lying plateau of Sacramento and vineyards."

Later in the day, the landscape changed dramatically again as they climbed up, up, to an altitude of some 8,500ft, over a high pass in the southerly reaches of the Sierra Nevada, a natural barrier along California's eastern border that was a major obstacle for the first settlers, and out over the vast desert wasteland that lay beyond. They touched down for the night in a remote dry river valley just to the east of the pass, still at some 6,000ft. Here they were on the fringes of the Mojave Desert, to the north and east of which lies Death Valley and Badwater Flat, a dazzling white salt flat which at 280ft below sea level makes it the lowest, hottest point in North America. Practiced campers by this point, Joanna and Steve had their tent pitched and a rack of lamb spitting on an open fire in minutes.

An early start followed. The two pilots were up and off before the heat of the day had a chance to build, destination Mojave, for fuel and water. Renowned for its role in aerospace history, Mojave is the home of the Rutan Voyager, the first aircraft to circumnavigate the world without stopping or refuelling.

Burt Rutan, designer of the Voyager, famously quipped that the isolation of the Mojave Desert is what fosters invention - there being little else to do. Rutan went on to design and launch SpaceShipOne, which won the Ansari X-Prize in 2004 for being the first privately funded spacecraft to fly into space twice within a two-week period.

Steve was fascinated by the place. Not so, Joanna. By 11 a.m. they had refuelled and were off, flying over mile upon mile of craggy, inhospitable desert hills.

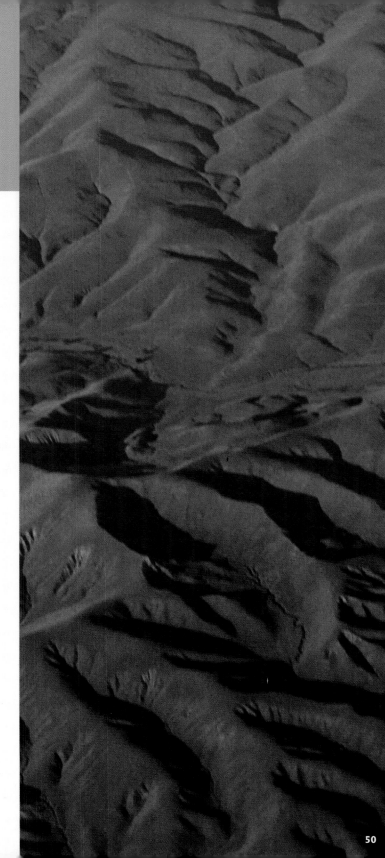

MOJAVE AIR AND SPACE PORT

For many visitors to the U.S., the allure of the Mojave Desert is to experience the natural wonders of the national parks it contains, in particular Death Valley and Joshua Tree. Or - for more worldly reasons - the gambling mecca of Las Vegas. But for flight test engineers and operators in the commercial and entrepreneurial space market, the Mojave Desert means just one thing: the Mojave Air and Space Port.

The airport - first opened in 1935 as a small, rural airfield serving the local gold and silver mining industry - is today, beside its role as a travel hub, a thriving, progressive hotbed of creativity. It has three main activities at its core: flight testing; maintenance and storage of aircraft; and space industry development. It is unique in being the only inland commercial spaceport, the first facility in the U.S. to be licensed for horizontal launches of reusable spacecraft, and the only spaceport from which there have been privately-funded human spaceflights.

Its location has a lot to do with it. Stuck out in the middle of the desert, there are few neighbours to complain about the roar of rocket engines. It's also high and dry, located at an elevation of nearly 2,800ft with fewer than 10 inches of rain a year - perfect for long-term storage of aircraft - while also offering consistently good visibility for experimental flights. Close to Edwards Air Force Base, it also has one other major advantage: airspace. The airspace overhead is a military operating area and the National Test Pilot School

based at Mojave has access to it, allowing pilots to fly straight up into a supersonic corridor.

Perhaps most important of all, however, is the attitude of the community that is drawn to it. "Mojave has an environment that supports rather than is afraid of experimental research testing," explains genius aerospace engineer, Burt Rutan. Noted for his originality in designing light, strong, quirky-looking, energy-efficient aircraft, Rutan has personally strapped himself in and tested a plane that has never been flown before on 38 occasions. "Those first flights are the things you remember as being the most fun, the most challenging, the most risky," he says, "and the reason we're in this. Flight test is our best card."

Rutan's many accomplishments include his design of the record-breaking Voyager, the first plane to circumnavigate the world without stopping or refuelling, and the sub-orbital SpaceShipOne, which won the Ansari X-Prize in 2004 for becoming the first privately-built and funded manned craft to enter the realm of space twice within two weeks.

Rutan is now working with Virgin Galactic, an offshoot of Sir Richard Branson's Virgin Group, to open up space tourism using spacecraft based on the designs of SpaceShipOne. Dubbed SpaceShipTwo, these new craft will allow six 'experience optimized' passengers to look down on the Earth from 70-80 miles up in suborbital space.

"The Mojave Space Port is the first facility in the U.S. to be licensed for horizontal launches of reusable spacecraft and the only spaceport from which there have been privately-funded human spaceflights."

ARIZONA

"The three horrid 'H's were at play: hot, high and humid. We were constantly climbing through piercing heat and we had to milk G-NUDE for every ounce of power."

If Joanna and Steve had not fully appreciated what it would be like to fly in scorching heat and high humidity, they were about to discover the truth as they approached Arizona. The state's climate is characterised by its mild winters and blazing, hot summers. During the latter, temperatures during the day can reach a blistering 50°C.

In what is primarily a desert landscape, Arizona is known for the huge variety of its topography including plateaus and mountains as well as huge swathes of desert plains. In addition to the Grand Canyon, many other national forests, parks, monuments, and Indian reservations are located in the state.

Their route, tracking south-east towards New Mexico, took them south of the Colorado Plateau over a region which despite the intense heat produces excellent crops. Arizona has one of the most efficient irrigation networks in the world with dams for water storage in lakes and reservoirs providing a large portion of the water for farming. From the air these irrigated crops stand out from the desert like huge discs of green against the arid desert around - crop circles indeed!

Flight Information

FLIGHT DISTANCE	283NM
FLIGHT TIME	2HRS 27MINS

ENTRY:N34° 54.30' W114° 37.68'.   EXIT:N35° 15.13' W109° 02.15'.

52

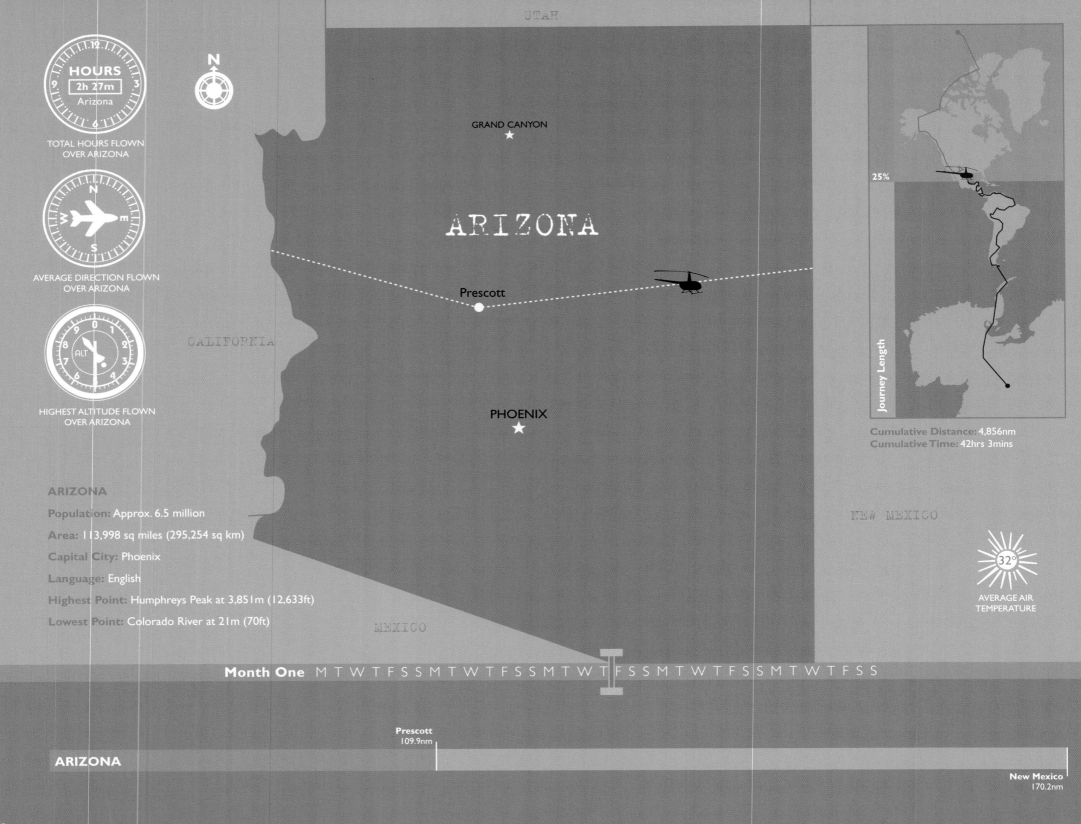

HOURS
2h 27m
Arizona

TOTAL HOURS FLOWN
OVER ARIZONA

AVERAGE DIRECTION FLOWN
OVER ARIZONA

ALT

HIGHEST ALTITUDE FLOWN
OVER ARIZONA

N

UTAH

GRAND CANYON
★

ARIZONA

Prescott

CALIFORNIA

PHOENIX
★

25%

Journey Length

Cumulative Distance: 4,856nm
Cumulative Time: 42hrs 3mins

NEW MEXICO

ARIZONA

Population: Approx. 6.5 million

Area: 113,998 sq miles (295,254 sq km)

Capital City: Phoenix

Language: English

Highest Point: Humphreys Peak at 3,851m (12,633ft)

Lowest Point: Colorado River at 21m (70ft)

MEXICO

32°

AVERAGE AIR
TEMPERATURE

Month One M T W T F S S M T W T F S S M T W T F S S M T W T F S S M T W T F S S

Prescott
109.9nm

ARIZONA

New Mexico
170.2nm

Diary

long day's flight in scorching heat, temperatures topping 44°C in the cockpit, and Joanna and Steve touched base at Prescott, Arizona. This county seat of Yavapai County is at an altitude of 5,400ft, and usually significantly cooler than the lower southern areas of the state, but on their day of arrival the temperature and humidity were running high.

By chance, at the airport, they met one of the instructors who had been on the Robinson training course in California a few weeks previously. He relayed his chilling story of dodging storms, lightning and a Chinook when coming into land. Conditions weren't looking favourable and Joanna's and Steve's plan was not to stay overnight but just re-fuel and move on. For the first time they experienced the joys of taking off with the three horrid 'H's at play: hot, high and humid.

"We had been warned not to take off over the buildings," says Joanna, "but didn't really take heed of this until we were on the runway. We could barely lift Nudie off the ground! The only way was to bounce her from skid to skid, scraping along the tarmac for the entire length of the runway before finally getting any lift. Luckily Steve was at the controls," she adds with characteristic modesty.

The weather failed to improve throughout the day. The landscape flying over Arizona was spectacular. This, one of the four corner states of North America, is dominated by forest, park land, and Native American reserves. It is most famous for the Grand Canyon - the biggest canyon in the world - carved out by the Colorado River to the north. But also for its desert landscape, rich in xerphyte plants such as cactus, and for its plains, plateaus and mountains.

It was these they flew over on their flight to New Mexico, brilliant in a spectrum of coppery colour. The only shadow cast over the splendor beneath them were the storm cells - great anvils of granite grey reaching from cloud to ground - building up all around them.

WHIRLYBIRD - A SHORT HISTORY OF THE HELICOPTER

"The idea of a vehicle that could lift itself vertically from the ground and hover motionless in the air was probably born at the same time that man dreamed of flying." So said Russian-born Igor Ivanovitch Sikorsky, widely acknowledged as the father of the helicopter, the inventor of the first successful helicopter upon which today's extraordinarily versatile and vital vehicles are based.

Sikorsky was indefatigable, a genius of aviation, but he was also blessed at being alive and working in the first half of the 20th century, following the invention of the internal combustion engine. For it was the development of an engine with adequate power to weight ratio that enabled pioneers to develop helicopters that could lift both machine and pilot off the ground.

For hundreds of years prior to this, humanity's dreams of flight had been inspired by the humming bird or dragon fly, or even the whirling, auto-rotating seeds of the sycamore carried on a breeze. As early as 400BC, the Chinese were making simple toys called Chinese Tops, comprising feathers at the end of a stick which could be spun between the hands to generate lift and fly.

In the 15th century, Leonardo de Vinci sketched a human-carrying Helical Aerial Screw, an elaboration of an Archimedes water-screw constructed from iron wire and starched linen. But this was essentially theoretical, never actually constructed.

There followed a series of inventions that made use of rubber bands, spindles or steam as a source of power, furthering the understanding of aerodynamics but doing nothing to lift man and machine off the ground. This was first accomplished by a French bicycle maker,

Paul Cornu, in 1907. His machine comprised a simple airframe with two rotors powered by a 24hp (18kw) gasoline motor and lifted its inventor a foot off the ground for all of 20 seconds, but was unstable and abandoned.

One of the major challenges of helicopter flight to overcome was the unequal lift produced on the rotor blades as they turned full circle, advancing and retreating from the relative wind in forward flight. This led to large oscillatory blade stresses at the rotor hub. Interestingly the solution was found by a man who never built a helicopter himself. In 1923, a Spaniard named Juan de la Cierva successfully flew his C4 autogiro, a hybrid aircraft with the wings and tail of a fixed-wing aeroplane and a rotor mounted on a vertical shaft above the fuselage.

The breakthrough was that the rotor blades weren't fixed, but effectively free - articulated - allowing each blade to flap, feather, lead or lag in response to the changing airloads during each blade revolution, and so compensate for dissymmetry of lift.

By 1936, many of the problems encountered had been overcome and the introduction of the German Focke-Wulf FW-61 with its twin rotors left and right of the fuselage marked the introduction of practical helicopter flight.

But it was Igor Ivanovitch Sikorsky, born in Russia but working in the U.S., who was to overcome the last major hurdle in the development of simpler, single-rotor helicopters. That hurdle was the torque produced by a single rotor. And the solution? A smaller rotor mounted vertically on the tail boom. To this day the VS-300 is the model upon which all single-rotor helicopters are based.

"A helicopter is an assembly of forty thousand loose pieces, flying more or less in formation."

NEW MEXICO

"The plains, plateaus and mountains were saturated in a brilliant copper colour. But storm cells, great anvils of granite grey, were building up all around us."

Adapting at last to the intense heat and the harsh beauty of the desert landscapes beneath them, Joanna and Steve headed south-east into New Mexico. As in Arizona, New Mexico is mostly desert with broad canvases of semi-arid plains flecked with the characteristic flora and fauna of the region - cacti, yucca, and desert grasses.

For Joanna, much of the attraction of the state lay in its history - a rich mix of traditions including Native American and Hispanic influences, the latter stretching back to when the region was part of the Spanish colonial empire. And nowhere does this potent mix bear more fruit than in the thriving cosmopolitan culture of the state capital, Santa Fe.

But further south, in the heart of the Tularosa Basin, they were to find themselves mesmerised by the massive gypsum dunes of the White Sands National Monument. These glistening white dunes of pure gypsum sand look like snowfields from afar and talcum powder close up and are one of the true wonders of the natural world.

Flight Information

FLIGHT DISTANCE	790NM
FLIGHT TIME	6HRS 50MINS

ENTRY:N35° 15.13′ W109° 02.15′.   EXIT:N32° 01.54′ W104° 34.39′.

HOURS

6h 50m
New Mexico

TOTAL HOURS FLOWN
OVER NEW MEXICO

N

AVERAGE DIRECTION FLOWN
OVER NEW MEXICO

HIGHEST ALTITUDE FLOWN
OVER NEW MEXICO

Population: Approx. 1,984,000

Area: 121,665 sq miles (315,194 sq km)

Capital City: Santa Fe

Languages: Spanish, English

Highest Point: Wheeler Peak at 4,011m (13,161ft)

Lowest Point: Red Bluff Reservoir at 866m (2,842ft)

ARIZONA

Durango

SANTA FE
Santa Fe Muncipal Airport

ALBUQUERQUE

NEW
MEXICO

Alamogordo White Sands

Las Cruces Intl

TEXAS

MEXICO

28%

Journey Length

Cumulative Distance: 5,647nm
Cumulative Time: 48hrs 53mins

40°

AVERAGE AIR
TEMPERATURE

Month One M T W T F S S M T W T F S S M T W T F S S M T W T F S S M T W T F S S

NEW MEXICO

Santa Fe Mun
145.7nm

Las Cruces Intl
294.6nm

Texas
86.8nm

Durango-La Plata Co
122.3nm

Alamogordo White Sands
57.5nm

" S torm cells are the one thing that can break an aircraft into pieces," says Steve. **"Definitely to be avoided."** Circumnavigating one and then another, Joanna and Steve finally arrived in New Mexico's capital, Santa Fe, at 7.30 p.m., and headed straight for a hotel. **"Fabulous to soak in a bath, after a couple of days camping in the desert,"** says Joanna.

Joanna experienced something refreshingly uplifting about Santa Fe. "It was Hispanic, vibrant. It had me reaching for my camera immediately," she says. A rich Native American culture in New Mexico, together with people of Spanish descent and Anglo-Americans, constitute a multi-cultural society unlike that of any other North American state. A large artistic and literary community thrives in Santa Fe, and there's a multitude

of museums and art galleries. But the pair's honeymoon was primarily a journey ever southwards and after a couple of day's relaxation, it was time to move on.

This time they were to experience a very different side to New Mexico. Due south 170 miles, a little way from Alamogordo in the mountain-ringed Tularosa Basin, lies the world's largest surface deposit of gypsum, the component mineral of plaster of Paris.

Gleaming gypsum crystals blown into massive dunes, as pure white as snow, engulf some 275 square miles of desert. Of this, 115 square miles is protected in the White Sands National Monument, while the remainder is military land.

Joanna and Steve parked G-NUDE at Alamogordo, hired a car, and drove to have a look. "There was a huge sign at the park entrance saying it would often

be closed for missile testing," says Joanna, "which we read to the roar of stealth bombers flying overhead."

The two of them walked for a couple of hours, away from any sign of man. "The sky was blue and the white sand had turned blue reflecting the sky," says Joanna. "We ran, and jumped, and kicked the sand like kids. It's so fine, almost like talcum powder." In this surreal world, they camped for the night.

"Some 275 square miles of gleaming gypsum crystals, blown into massive dunes as pure as driven snow."

DUNES OF GLISTENING WHITE SAND

Rising from the heart of the Tularosa Basin in south central New Mexico is one of the greatest natural wonders of the world: a glistening white dune field of pure gypsum sand that engulfs 275 square miles of desert. There are other pocket-sized gypsum fields around the world, but none on this scale.

Formal recognition of the uniqueness of these white sands came on January 18th, 1933, when President Herbert Hoover established White Sands National Monument. It comprises an area of 115 square miles of the southern part of the dune field with the aim of preserving its scenic beauty along with the plants and animals that have successfully adapted to living there. The remainder of the dune field is on military land not open to the public.

The formation of the gypsum sand dunes is in large part due to the distinctiveness of the surrounding topography. Gypsum, or hydrous calcium sulphate, the component mineral of common-or-garden plaster of Paris, is rarely found in the form of sand because it is water-soluble. Normally it would be dissolved in rain and carried out to sea.

But the Tularosa Basin is an internally drained valley; it has no outlet to the sea, and rain that dissolves gypsum from the surrounding San Andres and Sacramento mountains is trapped within the basin, either sinking into the ground or forming shallow pools which subsequently evaporate leaving gypsum in a crystalline form, called selenite, on the surface.

During the last ice age, much of the basin was covered with lakes, now dried out. In their place are the Alkali Flats and other dry lake beds covered in selenite crystals which, with weathering and erosion, have been broken down into sand and blown by the prevailing south-westerly winds into the magnificent wave-like dunes.

"Gypsum may be divided into two classes - commercial and inspirational," wrote Tom Charles, a local Alamogordo man and keen advocate for the formation of the White Sands National Monument in the 1920s and '30s. "The former everybody has, but as for recreational gypsum, we have it all. No place else in the world do you find these alabaster dunes with the beauty and splendour of the Great White Sands."

Almost a century on, the hundreds of thousands of people who visit White Sands National Monument every year are verification of his words. Visitors can drive into the dunes or explore them on marked trails by foot. Curiously, gypsum sand, unlike quartz-based sand, doesn't readily convert the sun's energy into heat and so can be walked upon safely with bare feet, even in the height of summer. Children frequently use the dunes for downhill sledding. For all visitors to the dunes, though, it is advisable to check on park closures before visiting. On average, it is closed a couple of times a week, for a period of one or two hours, while tests are conducted on the neighbouring White Sands Missile Range.

Another altogether more sinister landmark is not far off. On the northernmost boundaries of the Missile Range lies the Trinity site where the first atom bomb was detonated on 16th July, 1945.

"One of the greatest natural wonders of the world: a glistening white dune field of pure gypsum sand that engulfs 275 square miles of desert."

TEXAS

"The largest state in the U.S. Nearly 270,000 square miles in fact, and from up above it looked like there were oil wells everywhere."

Texas is renowned the world over for one characteristic above all others: its size. Everything in Texas, from the ranches and buildings to the burgers and ten gallon hats, is built to impress. Statistics often bore, but in the case of Texas they are jaw-dropping. To cater for its 16 million head of cattle, more than 110,000,000 acres of land are under pasture, almost double that of its nearest rival, Nevada.

Nothing that Steve and Joanna saw from the air was to change this pre-conceived impression. The size of the ranches underlined Texas's long-held position as the driving force behind the U.S. cattle industry and the thousands of 'nodding donkeys' - oil wells - was a clear demonstration of the state's extraordinary mineral wealth. What did surprise them both, however, was the discovery that Texas is also a world-leader in renewable energy producing more wind power than any other state in North America and with an even greater potential for solar energy in the future.

Flight Information

FLIGHT DISTANCE	664NM
FLIGHT TIME	5HRS 45MINS

ENTRY:N32° 01.54' W104° 34.39'. EXIT:N25° 51.80' W97° 27.81'.

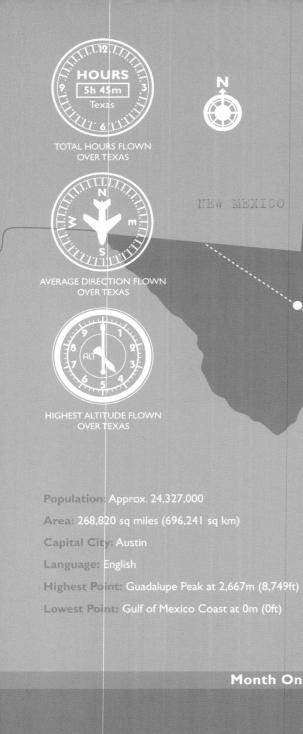

HOURS

5h 45m

Texas

TOTAL HOURS FLOWN
OVER TEXAS

N

AVERAGE DIRECTION FLOWN
OVER TEXAS

ALT

HIGHEST ALTITUDE FLOWN
OVER TEXAS

Population: Approx. 24,327,000

Area: 268,820 sq miles (696,241 sq km)

Capital City: Austin

Language: English

Highest Point: Guadalupe Peak at 2,667m (8,749ft)

Lowest Point: Gulf of Mexico Coast at 0m (0ft)

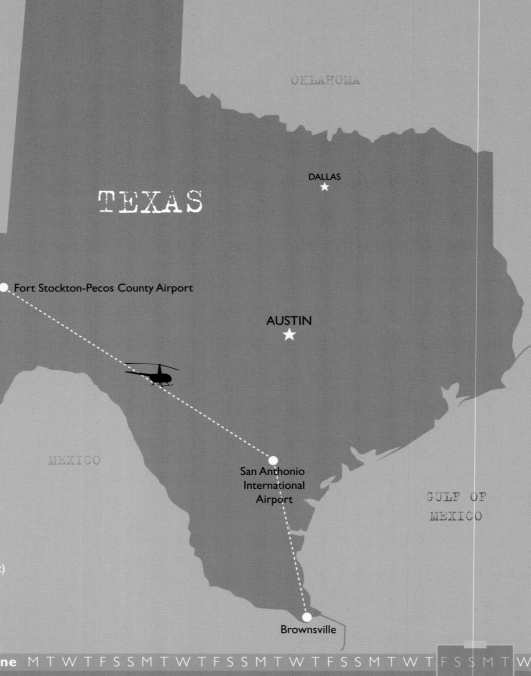

OKLAHOMA

NEW MEXICO

TEXAS

DALLAS ★

Fort Stockton-Pecos County Airport

AUSTIN ★

MEXICO

San Anthonio
International
Airport

GULF OF
MEXICO

Brownsville

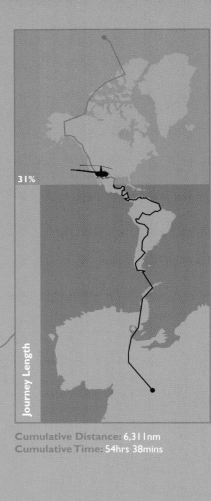

31%

Journey Length

Cumulative Distance: 6,311nm
Cumulative Time: 54hrs 38mins

40°

AVERAGE AIR
TEMPERATURE

Month One M T W T F S S M T W T F S S M T W T F S S M T W T F S S M T W T F S S

TEXAS

Fort Stockton-Pecos
107.8nm

Brownsville
224.6nm

San Antonio Intl
245nm

Mexico
3.3nm

Flying over Texas on the next leg of their journey, Steve and Joanna couldn't help but notice the abundance of oil wells - both used and unused. **"We flew over thousands of square miles of disused oil rig sites,"** says Steve, **"just concrete pads where once there'd been nodding donkeys. As well as** **active ones, too, of course,"** he adds.

Before long, the two pilots were approaching the U.S./Mexican border landing at Matamoros, just seven miles into Mexico. As usual when entering a new country, they cleared customs and immigration, paid their dues for fuel and service, and then jumped aboard the helicopter.

But suddenly, unexpectedly, the brakes were applied. A radio call from the control tower instructed them to return to the commandant's office. There, in sweltering heat, they waited three hours while the commandant repeatedly insisted they didn't have the appropriate paperwork and that, being Saturday, there wasn't a lot he could do about it.

This is the short version. The long version involves emails and faxes flying across oceans as tempers flared to match the heat outside. "Suddenly," says Steve, "it was apparent we couldn't simply fly in and out of countries at will. It felt like we'd hit a brick wall."

In the end they were obliged to fly back to Brownsville in the U.S.

"We had no choice," says Steve. "We realised we had completely underestimated what we were doing, and that we had to totally change our way of thinking to move forward."

In practice, this meant countless hours on trans-Atlantic calls to Overflight in the U.K. who had been helping them with flight planning and customs clearance. But it also meant a shift in the pilots' approach to bureaucracy on their own part.

"We needed to stop and spend a day or two organising ourselves," says Joanna, "to ensure every detail of the paperwork was in order: flight plans, entry points to different countries, re-fuelling points. All very tedious, but absolutely essential."

TEXAS - PIONEER OF WIND POWER

Texas, once the oil capital of the U.S., still accounts for about quarter of the country's known oil reserves. Surprisingly to some, though, it is now also rapidly becoming a leader in renewable energy sources, producing more wind power than any other state in the nation. Travel the length of this vast southern state and the view is as likely to be of immense wind turbines silhouetted against the skyline as it is of oil rigs.

For centuries, local communities have harnessed the wind's energy to grind corn, pump water, and propel boats, but in a post-industrial age wind turbines have been a marginal form of electrical generation. Until now. In recent years, advancements in technology and a rising concern about greenhouse gases, coupled with government incentives and high fuel prices, have propelled the U.S. to step on the wind power accelerator. Currently the U.S. is the fastest growing wind power market in the world, albeit from a small base, and over half its growth is contributed by Texas.

Wind energy accounts for more than three per cent of all energy used in Texas - that's enough to supply a million homes - and is growing, while large portions of wind energy generated also go to markets in other states. Across the U.S., wind power supplies about one per cent of electricity, powering the equivalent of four-and-a-half million homes. Environmental advocates declare it could eventually hit 20 per cent, as has already happened in Denmark, while energy consultants tend to be more conservative, suggesting five to seven per cent as realistic.

Whichever scenario proves the case in the long term, there are several forces working to the advantage of wind power in Texas. For one, it is windy. The Texas Panhandle, along the Gulf Coast south of Galveston, and in the mountain passes and ridge tops of the Trans-Pecos are some of the windiest spots in the Americas.

It also has sparsely populated land for wind farms and, importantly, a friendly regulatory environment for developers. Generally, there is wide acknowledgment that the wind power industry can create jobs and help maintain long-term employment for many years after the rigs stop producing oil. The farmers, too, can significantly boost their income by leasing their land to wind developers.

Wind power has a long history in Texas. West Texas State University began wind energy research in 1970 which led to the formation of the Alternative Energy Institute in 1977. And in Texas everything comes big - including its wind farms. The Horse Hollow Wind Energy Centre is the largest wind farm in the world with a total capacity of 735 megawatts spread across 47,000 acres in Taylor and Nolan counties, and there are a couple of others under construction that will be bigger still.

Wind power has its limitations, of course. Electricity from wind remains costlier than that generated from fossil fuels - though the gap is closing - and it can be intermittent and unpredictable. Also, the turbines are getting bigger and their blades can kill bird and bats. Wildlife and aesthetic issues have led to some opposition across the country, particularly in coastal areas such as Cape Cod, but in Texas the opposition has been limited and has done little to slow the rapid growth of wind power.

Many see the sleek new turbines as a welcome change in the landscape, an improvement over the oil and gas rigs which have dominated the landscape for so long. Texas is top of the American league in wind power and the hope is that it will stay that way for a long time to come.

"Many see the sleek new turbines as a welcome change, an improvement over the oil and gas rigs of the last 100 years."

CENTRAL AMERICA

Central America is a bridge, both geographically and culturally, between two very different continents. Even after all their adventures to date, Joanna and Steve were still taken aback by the explosion of colour that greeted them as they burst across the border into Latin America.

MEXICO ▸ BELIZE ▸ GUATEMALA ▸ HONDURAS ▸ NICARAGUA ▸ COSTA RICA ▸ PANAMA

MEXICO

"The colour and warmth of Latin America hit us like an express train. Suddenly there was colour and vitality everywhere."

Their route across Mexico took them down the east coast adjacent to the Gulf of Mexico where they made a stop-over at a small hotel close to the shore of Lake Catemaco, an area known for its association with witchcraft going back many centuries.

From here they headed out over the sea to Villahermosa and to Merida on the Yucatán peninsula. Here they were to view from the air the ancient Mayan civilization which dominated the region before the arrival of the Spanish conquistadors in the 16th century.

The Mayan empire once covered the whole of south-eastern Mexico and parts of Guatemala, Honduras, Belize and El Salvador and their magnificent aerial view of Chichén Itzá was their first encounter with the many architectural wonders of this ancient world.

Flight Information

FLIGHT DISTANCE	963NM
FLIGHT TIME	8HRS 20MINS

ENTRY:N25° 51.80' W97° 27.81'.   EXIT:N18° 29.36' W88° 26.40'.

HOURS
8h 20m
Mexico

TOTAL HOURS FLOWN
OVER MEXICO

AVERAGE DIRECTION FLOWN
OVER MEXICO

HIGHEST ALTITUDE FLOWN
OVER MEXICO

NEW MEXICO

MEXICO

Gen Servando Canales
International Airport

GULF OF
MEXICO

Tampico

Gen Heriberto Jara
International Airport

Lic
Manuel Crecencio

Chichén-Itzá

MEXICO CITY

Swimming Beach

Catemaco   Villahermosa

BELIZE

GUATEMALA

36%

Journey Length

Cumulative Distance: 7,274nm
Cumulative Time: 62hrs 58mins

Population: Approx. 109,956,000

Area: 758,449 sq miles (1,964,375 sq km)

Capital City: Mexico City

Language: Spanish

Highest Point: Volcan Pico de Orizaba at 5,700m (18,701ft)

Lowest Point: Laguna Salada at -10m (-33ft)

35°

AVERAGE AIR
TEMPERATURE

Month One M T W T F S S M T W T F S S M T W T F S S M T W T F S S M T W T F S S

Gen Servando Canales Intl
6.5nm

MEXICO

Tampico
209.8nm

Gen Heriberto Jara Intl
210.8nm

Catemaco
78.8nm

Villahermosa
128.9nm

Swimming Beach
87.9nm

Lic Manuel Crecencio
166.7nm

Chichen-Itza
70.2nm

Belize
129.1nm

t was August 5th, 2002, and at last they felt confident to cross the Mexican border and attempt to clear customs at Matamoros once again. They were greeted by the same commandant as before, though on this occasion, he swiftly retrieved their paperwork from a safe, made a couple of calls and, within moments, confirmed their status, all with apparent ease.

The problem was solved, and Joanna and Steve were free to continue their journey. Many have claimed Mexico to be a traveller's paradise, a country, vast in size, with a multitude of identities: deserts and snow-capped volcanoes, ancient ruins and industrialized cities, time-warped colonial towns and glitzy resorts.

The pilots' path took them along the east coast, hugging the Gulf of Mexico, with stops at Tampico and Veracruz to file flight plans and refuel. They stopped for the night at a small hotel close to the shore of Lagunas de Catemaco, a lake surrounded by the volcanic peaks of Sierra de Los Tuxtlas, and infamous, so legend has it, for 'brujos' or witches.

"It was a magical day," says Joanna, "flying over lush countryside and along miles of coastline. When we were hungry, we stopped at a tiny fishing village in the hope of buying some fish, and met some delightful fishermen who happily prepared us some lunch. And then we flew inland, over undulating verdant hills - Hobbit's Kingdom, we called it - before making a long circuit of Lagunas de Catemaco in the fading light."

It was hot here in Mexico, air temperatures rising to 38°C.

But flying helicopters affords a sort of freedom that other modes of transport deny. When the temperature became too hot for comfort, Joanna and Steve, spotting an idyllic, deserted beach, landed G-NUDE and took a dip. Then with bodies wet and clothes abandoned, they took off with the 'organic air-conditioning' switched on, as Joanna puts it.

Their destination that evening, suitably attired once more, was the president's suite at the luxurious 17th century, Hacienda Katanchel. This was a honeymoon after all! Located in the heart of what used to be a sisal plantation close to the old colonial town of Mérida, on the Yucatán peninsula, Hacienda Katanchel is one of the region's most prestigious properties. It had been exquisitely restored and converted into a hotel by husband and wife team, Anibal González and Mónica Hernández.

As hard as they searched, though, repeatedly circling where they presumed it to be, they couldn't find it. Admitting defeat, they headed for the airport at Mérida and parked

G-NUDE before hiring a VW Beetle and searching again. Again they were lost for an hour, before finally stumbling upon the hacienda, set deep in the dripping, verdant rainforest. "It was just fabulous," says Steve. "A donkey towed our bags along an old railway track to our room in a converted sisal shed. Tranquil gardens, a first class restaurant - it offered a real sense of the history of Spanish colonial times."

Their night of luxury at the hacienda was their last in Mexico before flying south over the Yucatán peninsula, detouring to enjoy a bird's eye view of the Mayan ruins of Chichén Itzá, and then flying a couple of hundred miles over rainforest, storm cells building all the way to Belize.

"When the temperature became too hot for comfort, Joanna and Steve landed G-NUDE on an idyllic, deserted beach and took a dip. Then, with bodies wet and clothes abandoned, took off again with the 'organic air-conditioning' switched on."

ANCIENT CIVILIZATIONS - THE MAYA AND THE AZTECS

Today's Mexico is a fascinating, diverse country, rich in intrigue for the urbanite and nature-lover alike. But more intriguing still are the remnants of yesterday's Mexico: the wondrous archaeological sites of the pre-Columbian Maya and Aztec civilizations dotted across the width and breadth of the country.

The Maya is a Mesoamerican civilization, noted for its fully developed written language - the only one of pre-Columbian America - as well as for its art, architecture, advanced mathematics and astronomy. Initially established during the pre-Classic period (c. 2000BC to 250AD), many Mayan cities burst forth in scale and sophistication during the Classic period (c. 250AD to 900AD) and continued throughout the post-Classic period until the arrival of the Spanish.

At its peak, it was one of the most densely populated and culturally dynamic societies in the world, extending throughout what are now the southern states of Mexico and the Yucatán peninsula, as well as Guatemala, Belize, El Salvador and western Honduras. To this day, the Maya form sizeable populations through the region, holding on to many of the traditions of their pre-Columbian forebears, although usually mixed with post-conquest Catholicism.

Ancient architectural sites of the Maya civilization in today's Mexico are numerous including famous examples like Chichén-Itzá, Palenque, Tulum, Uxmal and Kabah. Each is unique, built as dictated by the topography, sprawling across the plains of northern Yucatán, perched atop a hill or, as in the case of Tulum, on a cliff top overlooking the Caribbean. Each also has certain features in common with the others including a north-south orientation, paved ceremonial plazas, palaces, ball courts, and most strikingly, stepped pyramids with small temples on top, at least as spectacular as anything in ancient Greece or Rome.

Those interested in the Aztecs, the Nahuatal speaking peoples who controlled the Valley of Mexico and much of Central America from the 14th century until the Spanish invasion of the 16th century, need look no further than the Mexican capital itself. Mexico City was built on the ruins of Tenochtitlan, the capital of the Aztec Empire. As recently as 1978, an Aztec carving was discovered in the heart of the city which prompted extensive excavations and the discovery of the ruined Templo Mayor, once a massive stone pyramid with twin temples dedicated to Huitzilopochtli, the god of war, and Tlaloc, the rain god.

It was built sometime after 1325 AD, on this particular spot according to Aztec sources, because of an eagle that was seen perched on a cactus devouring a snake - the fulfilment of a prophecy - and was the centre of religious life for some 300,000 people until it was destroyed by the Spanish in 1521.

Human sacrifices to appease the gods were a frequent event on the pyramid, the victims killed with an obsidian knife on a high altar and ceremoniously thrown down the staircase. For many, human sacrifice is the most striking feature of Aztec civilization and while it was practiced throughout Mesoamerica, the Aztecs, if their own accounts are to be believed, brought the practice to an unprecedented level.

According to the writings of the Franciscan monk, Bernardino de Sahagún, Aztecs informants defended the practice by asserting that it was not very different from the European way of waging warfare: Europeans killed the warriors in battle; Aztecs killed the warriors after the battle.

"Every site has certain features in common including a north-south orientation, paved ceremonial plazas, palaces, ball courts, and most strikingly, stepped pyramids with small temples on top. At least as spectacular as anything in ancient Greece or Rome."

BELIZE

"We were back in sand and palm trees territory. Not that we were complaining. And aboard our flying carpet we could pull up wherever the fancy took!"

Joanna's and Steve's flight south through Central America was remarkable for many exotic tropical landscapes, none more so than the barrier reef which runs parallel with the coast of Belize like a coral necklace for nearly 200 miles. Just one section of the largest barrier reef in the northern hemisphere, it is famous for its offshore atolls, blue holes, mangrove forests and coastal lagoons.

The reef is also home to hundreds of off-lying sand islands known as Cayes (pronounced 'keys'), some inhabited and some not, which are a magnet for a huge diversity of coral and marine life as well as the thousands of tourists who come for the world-class opportunities to snorkel and dive.

Generally trying to avoid tourist hot-spots, Joanna and Steve were nonetheless enchanted by Caye Caulker, a coral island measuring no more than five miles long and one mile wide. Revelling in the sun and the intense shades of the Caribbean Sea, there was at last time to enjoy a bit of real honeymooning after all.

Flight Information

| FLIGHT DISTANCE | 230NM |
| FLIGHT TIME | 2HRS |

ENTRY: N18° 29.36' W88° 26.40'.   EXIT: N17° 19.28' W88° 07.48'.

TOTAL HOURS FLOWN
OVER BELIZE

N

AVERAGE DIRECTION FLOWN
OVER BELIZE

HIGHEST ALTITUDE FLOWN
OVER BELIZE

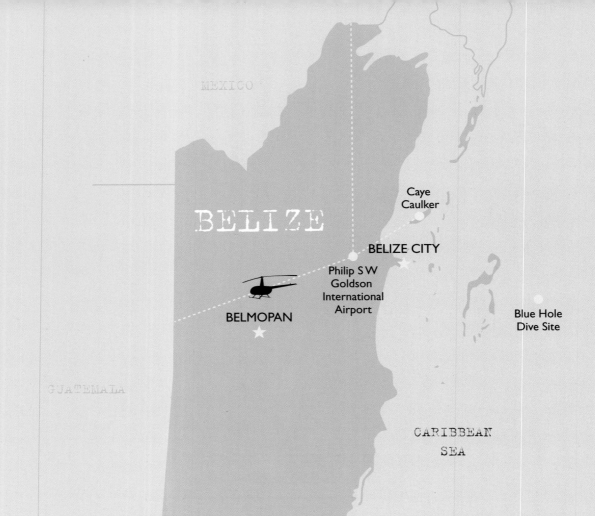

MEXICO

BELIZE

Caye
Caulker

BELIZE CITY

Philip S W
Goldson
International
Airport

BELMOPAN

Blue Hole
Dive Site

GUATEMALA

CARIBBEAN
SEA

HONDURAS

Population: Approx. 301,300

Area: 8,867 sq miles (22,966 sq km)

Capital City: Belmopan

Languages: Spanish, Belizean Kriol

Highest Point: Victoria Peak at 1,160m (3,806ft)

Lowest Point: Caribbean Sea at 0m (0ft)

37%

Journey Length

Cumulative Distance: 7,503nm
Cumulative Time: 64hrs 58mins

32°

AVERAGE AIR
TEMPERATURE

Month One M T W T F S S M T W T F S S M T W T F S S M T W T F S S M T W T F S S

BELIZE

Philip S W Goldson Intl
57.5nm

Philip S W Goldson Intl
21.3nm

Caye Caulker
21.6nm

Guatemala
48.5nm

As if violent weather and building storm clouds during the flight across the border weren't worry enough, they instantly hit another bureaucratic nightmare. But now with one added obstacle thrown in: private helicopters, they were told, are not permitted to fly in Belize airspace.

And certainly not to Cay Caulker, a small limestone coral island off the coast where they'd hoped to relax for a few days, soak up the sun, and perhaps indulge in a spot of scuba diving. They'd hit this brick wall before, though, and with fast mounting experience were better equipped to knock it down, or at least clamber over it.

An hour of gentle coaxing and they were granted permission to fly, and became the first people ever to land a private helicopter on Cay Caulker. Here, with no pressing need to hurry, they locked up G-NUDE, kicked off their shoes and joined the international band of barefoot backpackers, windsurfers and scuba divers intent on enjoying a paradise island of white coral sand.

Steve even fulfilled an ambition to dive the infamous Great Blue Hole, a perfectly circular underwater sinkhole that plunges to depths of 400ft. "I went a bit deeper than I meant to and got a bit narced," Steve confesses. "I just wanted to hug the stalactites and feed my compressed air to the fish!"

"Locking up G-NUDE, they joined the international band of backpackers, windsurfers and scuba-divers on a bar of pure, white coral sand."

BELIZE BARRIER REEF

The Belize Barrier Reef is a series of coral reefs stretching for some 170 miles off the coast of Belize. It is just part of the 600-mile Mesoamerican Barrier Reef which is the largest coral reef system in the world after the Great Barrier Reef in Australia. Fly south from Mexico and you will see the reef as an unbroken chain of white surf running along the Caribbean coast of the Yucatán peninsula and continuing south almost the whole length of the country to the Ranguana and Sapodilla Cays - a paradise for snorkellers and scuba-divers.

The Barrier Reef grows along the edge of the continent's shelf, separated from the mainland by a stunningly clear and shallow, turquoise-tinted lagoon. Outside the reef, the sea floor falls sharply in a series of plateaus to depths of over 3,000ft and from the air the colour of the sea is a dark royal blue. At the southern end of Belize, the reef is as much as 25 miles offshore, while in the north it is only a few hundred yards from land and, unusually, actually touches the shoreline at Rocky Point - one of the few sites in the world where a major barrier reef meets the coast.

A further unusual phenomenon is the presence of three separate atoll reefs to the east of the Barrier Reef: Tuneffe, Glover's, and furthest east, Lighthouse Reef. Atolls such as these are extremely rare in the Caribbean, and are more commonly found in the Pacific where they form on the top of submerged volcanoes. These three off the coast of Belize lie on non-volcanic submarine ridges. Perhaps unsurprisingly, considering its extraordinary natural beauty, the reef is Belize's top tourist destination with the coral cays, Cay Caulker, and the largest most northerly cay, Ambergris, being particularly popular with visitors. The diving is among the best

in the world. Coral reefs are home to more species than any other marine ecosystem - only rainforest rank higher on the biodiversity scale - and Belize has particularly high species diversity for the region. Rainbow tinged tropical fish, delicate sea fans and majestic coral gardens abound.

And for thrill-seekers, 60 miles offshore is one of the most outstanding dive sites on Earth. Like a giant pupil in a sea of turquoise, the Great Blue Hole is a perfectly circular limestone sinkhole over 325 yards in diameter and 130 yards deep, where on occasions divers can enjoy the company of nurse sharks, reef sharks, and even bull sharks and hammerheads.

In many ways the most fascinating aspect of the reef, though, is the coral itself. It is easy to forget, if observed only during the daylight hours, that it is a living wall formed by millions of coral organisms - soft, tube-shaped, carnivorous polyps which at night, capture small sea creatures with stinging tentacles. During the day, the organisms draw their tentacles into a hard layer of calcium carbonate called a corallite which en masse form into elaborate shapes from which they get their names. Hence brain coral, stag horn coral and elk horn coral.

In recognition of its importance as a natural habitat for such a huge array of species, much of the reef is protected by the Belize Barrier Reef Resource System and is designated a World Heritage Site. Nonetheless, the reef - not an inanimate lump of stone but a sensitive, living ecosystem - continues to show signs of stress from life in the modern world: oceanic pollution, shipping, fishing and tourism all taking their toll. Hurricanes and climate change also pose a threat and scientists claim that since 1998, more than 40 per cent of Belize's coral reef has been damaged.

"The Barrier Reef grows along the edge of the continent's shelf, separated from the mainland by a stunningly clear and shallow, turquoise-tinted lagoon."

GUATEMALA

"Such amazing vibrancy in such a poor country. We were just blown away by the people and the richness of the culture. The sense of enjoyment in life was everywhere."

If the colour and vibrancy of Mexico had immediately assaulted their senses as they flew south into Central America, how much more was this true in Guatemala. Their first immediate goal was to fly south-west from their idyllic few days on the Caribbean coast of Belize to seek out Tikal, another of the lost wonders of the Mayan universe.

Of all the 'Lost Cities' of the pre-Colombian world, Tikal is perhaps the most enigmatic. Unlike the cities of Chichén Itzá and Palenque on the Yucatán peninsula in Mexico, its remote location in the north of Guatemala makes it more difficult for tourists to reach, and much of it is still swamped by the forest which first began its relentless assault when the city was abandoned around 900 AD.

But while the Maya themselves only now exist in the imagination, the colour and vibrancy of their world can still be found further south in the vibrant communities of their descendants who still live around Lake Atitlán. And it was here during a magical few days break from their aerial odyssey that Joanna was able to let loose with her camera on terra firma once more.

Flight Information

FLIGHT DISTANCE	285NM
FLIGHT TIME	2HRS 27MINS

ENTRY:N17° 19.28' W88° 07.48'.   EXIT:N15° 10.03' W88° 57.77'.

86

HOURS
2h 27m
Guatemala

TOTAL HOURS FLOWN
OVER GUATEMALA

AVERAGE DIRECTION FLOWN
OVER GUATEMALA

HIGHEST ALTITUDE FLOWN
OVER GUATEMALA

N

GUATEMALA

TIKAL NATIONAL PARK

General De Brigada
Flores

MEXICO

BELIZE

CARIBBEAN
SEA

Casa Posado

GUATEMALA CITY

LAGO DE ATITLÁN

La Aurora Intl

HONDURAS

Population: Approx. 13,002,000

Area: 42,042 sq miles (108,890 sq km)

Capital City: Guatemala City

Language: Spanish

Highest Point: Volcano Tajumulco at 4,211m (13,816ft)

Lowest Point: Pacific Ocean at 0m (0ft)

NORTH
PACIFIC
OCEAN

EL SALVADOR

Journey Length

39%

Cumulative Distance: 7888nm
Cumulative Time: 67hrs 25mins

35°

AVERAGE AIR
TEMPERATURE

Month Two S S M T W T F S S M T W T F S S M T W T F S S M T W T F S S M T W T F S S

General De Brigada, Flores
49.4nm

La Aurora Intl
34.9nm

GUATEMALA

Casa Posado
152.7nm

Honduras
97.2nm

hree days later, August 11th, they took to the air once more, this time in a south-westerly direction over the Belize border into Guatemala, to catch a glimpse of Tikal, the largest of the ancient ruined cities of the Maya civilization.

"It was our first real experience of flying over rainforest," says Steve, "and it very quickly became apparent why they are called 'rainforests'. It started to rain; torrential rain, a downpour. Water was seeping into the cabin through the window seals and the vents. We realised pretty quickly that we'd have to abandon any

pre-conceived European concept of a forest. In Central America, a forest isn't a wooded area, it's a wooded landmass!

"It stretched as far as we could see with dark, vertical clouds, like pillars hanging on the canopy. We'd grown used to the idea that if we had a problem in the air, we could land,"

Steve adds, "but in the rainforest this safety blanket was worthless. The game had been raised again." "Yet," adds Joanna, "it was stunningly beautiful, even mystical. We were flying just above the tree tops and the canopy unfolded before us like the waves in an ocean. Then, suddenly, on the horizon, the towers of Tikal rose above the

trees, like a liner at sea, enshrouded in mist."

Though doubtless privileged to view Tikal's pyramids and palaces from the sky, Joanna and Steve couldn't land a helicopter in what is a national park, and flew on to land at the airport at Flores, before jumping on a bus back to Tikal for a closer

look. "Thick fog at dawn," says Joanna, "but still heavy with atmosphere."

From Flores, they flew south to Guatemala City, and west, through the terraced volcanic hills of the Guatemalan Highlands, to what Aldous Huxley considered the most beautiful of all the lakes in

the world. "Lake Como, it seems to me, touched the limit of the permissibly picturesque," he wrote, "but Atitlán is Como with the additional embellishments of several immense volcanoes. It really is too much of a good thing."

Lago de Atitlán is also the deepest lake in Central America, its turquoise waters reaching to depths of more than 1,100ft; and dotted around its shores are towns and villages in which Mayan culture is prevalent to this day, and traditional dress the norm.

Joanna and Steve circled its perimeter, marvelling at the ever-changing shades of its mercurial waters, unsure where they might land. Then, on a small grassy ledge perched high above the water's edge hardly bigger than a tennis court, they spotted two 'H's marking the site of two helicopter landing pads.

"We landed," says Steve, "and a butler came to greet us." It was the helipad for the Hotel Casa Posado at Santa Catarina Palopó - an accidental find that, in the view of our two travelling honeymooners, was the most enchanting hotel of the trip, and a perfect resting spot from which to explore the rich cultural communities dotted about the lake.

Joanna couldn't resist it. Cocktails and Condé Naste chic have their place, but a taxi ride would take her to the highland market town of Sololá, perched high above the lake, where virtually all the residents are Kaqchikal Mayas, proud to retain their heritage intact. It was an interest in the colour and diversity of cultures that was later to lead her to study social anthropology at The School of Oriental and African Studies in London. But here she could witness the Maya people and

their traditional way of life with her own eyes.

Up with the light, she kissed a sleepy Steve goodbye, grabbed her camera, and travelled the only tarmac road to Sololá. "There was some sort of fiesta underway," says Joanna. "There were hundreds of children, the boys dressed in cropped, cream-coloured jackets with intricate embroidery on the back, and the girls wrapped in seemingly layer upon layer of heavy, brightly-coloured woven cloth, all forming a procession through the streets, beating drums, playing trumpets and waving balloons."

It was no surprise to learn later that Sololá's major festival, Nim Jij Sololá, is celebrated annually on August 16th, just two days after she was there. "There was an amazing market as well," Joanna adds, "where crowds from communities around the lake gathered to sell tomatoes, chickens, squash, beans and pumpkins; and both men and women wore traditional dress."

A bus ride from Sololá took Joanna to Panajachel, the largest of the towns on the shores of Lago de Atitlán, which in contrast to Sololá has been overwhelmed by tourists over the years. In the 1960s it was hippies it attracted and although the war caused many foreigners to leave, the end of hostilities in 1996 saw visitor numbers boom again and today its economy is almost entirely reliant on tourism.

Joanna fleetingly walked its streets and took a cab once more, back to the luxury of Casa Posado for a late breakfast and a snooze. In the afternoon, this time together, Joanna and Steve ventured out to San Antonia Palopó, another of the lakeside towns, linked by a single tarmac road through Santa

Catarina Palopó. Here the women used traditional back-strap looms and brilliantly coloured cloth and locally-made ceramics were on sale. But, temptingly beautiful as they may have been, none could be bought so tight was the space in G-NUDE.

The next morning, on the move again, Joanna and Steve prepared to lift off from the hotel helipad - an undertaking that might have proved challenging under normal circumstances considering the diminutive size of the helipad. On this particularly day it was nothing short of hair-raising due to the Bell 206 Jet Ranger helicopter parked immediately adjacent to theirs.

A closer look revealed some savage looking wires overhead and the three horrid 'H's were also at play: they were 6,600ft high; the heat was 30°C and rising; and it was humid - a combination resulting in a density altitude of around 9,500ft.

"It was fairly advanced flying," says Steve, who was at the controls. "He lifted Nudie into a hover," continues Joanna. "All well, so we took a deep breath and climbed over the top of the Jet Ranger, and up again - steady climb - then swooped over the wire, before diving to pick up speed and flying out over the water. Amazing!"

This wasn't the only occasion they were to hold their breath in flight that day. Later, following a brief stop at Guatemala City, a delay of a couple of hours triggered a series of events that might well have ended in disaster. Maybe they shouldn't have flown on from the city at all, considering the two hours lost for the onward journey, but such are the pressures to stick within the time parameters of a pre-scheduled flight plan, that such speculation can be dismissed with the simple phrase: "easy to say in hindsight".

"There were hundreds of children: the boys dressed in cropped, cream-coloured jackets; the girls wrapped in layer upon layer of brightly-coloured woven cloth."

"We'd grown used to the idea that if we had a problem we could land," remembers Steve. "But in the rainforest this safety blanket was worthless. The game had been raised again."

TIKAL NATIONAL PARK

Tikal, in the Peten region of northern Guatemala, is the largest of the ancient ruined cities of the Maya civilization. It is Guatemala's cultural jewel. In its heyday, Tikal is believed to have been home to some 90,000 inhabitants and was one of the largest and most populated cities of the Late Classic Period of the Maya world.

But after 900 AD, when the Classic Maya civilization in the southern Maya lowlands collapsed, it was abruptly abandoned, remaining hidden for centuries as its temples and palaces were slowly strangled by the subtropical rainforest in which it lies.

All that survived was a legend among the descendants of the Maya which told of a lost city and a civilization in which their ancestors had achieved a high intellectual and artistic sophistication characterized by magnificent architecture, sculpture and paintings, complex writing and numerical systems, and an astronomical knowledge surpassing anything in Europe at the time. Then, in 1848, legend turned to fact when Ambrosio Tut, a gum-sapper, climbing high in a sapodilla tree, spotted the characteristic roof combs of the city's temples standing tall above the forest canopy in the distance.

Today, the Tikal National Park, designated a UNESCO World Heritage Site, comprises 222 square miles of rainforest around the ceremonial heart. Under the auspices of the University of Pennsylvania, it took 13 years - from 1956 to 1969 - to study and excavate 10 square miles of it. Research continues today under the auspices of the Proyecto Nacional Tikal University of San Carlos

in Guatemala and the Instituto de Antropología e Historia, unveiling more wonders with each passing year.

Studies have uncovered the location of more than 4,000 structures, many of which have been excavated, and some - including the Great Plaza, the North Acropolis, the Central Acropolis and various twin-pyramid complexes - restored. Vegetation still obliterates many of the urban spaces of this once vibrant city, but viewing points retrieved from the grip of the forest allow visitors to imagine how the ancient city must have looked over a millennium ago with its towering temples ablaze in bright colours, billowing smoke rising from a multitude of censers, and dense crowds going about their business in the plazas and avenues below.

Scholars have determined that the original settlers arrived in Tikal as early as 800BC, and have been able to trace their activities through changes in style, ceramics and architecture, through to the collapse of the Maya world in 900AD.

It was once believed that the Maya were a peaceful people concerned with spiritual growth and astronomical observations, but recent studies have revealed something quite different. Living in city states, like Tikal, and exercising domination over large tracts of territory, they controlled trade routes and collected taxes under a complex political system led by a dynastic Halach Huinic, or Sacred Lord. Inscriptions on altars in Tikal tell the story of a dynastic succession of Halach Huinic who presided over the destiny of their people based on a belief in an absolute divine power.

"In 1848, Ambrosio Tut, a gum-sapper, climbing high in a sapodilla tree, spotted the characteristic roof combs of Tikal's temples standing tall above the forest canopy."

HONDURAS

"We were in the tropics now and no mistake. The flying was very demanding with dense cloud rising from the rainforest beneath."

Flying east from Guatemala City, Joanna and Steve were soon heading over the border into northern Honduras. Once again they found themselves over a vast area of dense rainforest. Beneath them was the Pico Bonito National Park, recognised as one of Central America's biodiversity hotspots due to the numerous plant and animal species found in the region.

Protected areas in northern Honduras are part of the Mesoamerican Biological Corridor (MBC), a concept of sustainable development bringing together goals of conservation with the initiatives of local peoples throughout the region.

While from the air the beauty of the jungle beneath was undeniable, the navigational problems caused by towering accumulations of thunder cloud had some unforeseen, and potentially fatal, consequences.

At one point they were to find themselves seriously off course with diminishing amount of landing space and the prospect of a night landing ahead.

Flight Information

FLIGHT DISTANCE	290NM
FLIGHT TIME	2HRS 31MINS

ENTRY: N15° 10.03' W88° 57.77'.   EXIT: N13° 46.93' W86° 34.19'.

HOURS
2h 31m
Honduras

TOTAL HOURS FLOWN
OVER HONDURAS

AVERAGE DIRECTION FLOWN
OVER HONDURAS

HIGHEST ALTITUDE FLOWN
OVER HONDURAS

N

GUATEMALA

CARIBBEAN
SEA

Goloson International Airport

Night Valley

La Mesa
International
Airport

HONDURAS

TEGUCIGALPA

NICARAGUA

CARIBBEAN
SEA

Population: Approx. 7,639,000

Area: 43,278 sq miles (112,492 sq km)

Capital City: Tegucigalpa

Language: Spanish

Highest Point: Cerro Las Minas at 2,870m (9,416ft)

Lowest Point: Caribbean Sea at 0m (0ft)

41%

Journey Length

Cumulative Distance: 8,078nm
Cumulative Time: 69hrs 56mins

33°

AVERAGE AIR
TEMPERATURE

Month Two S S M T W T F S S M T W T F S S M T W T F S S M T W T F S S M T W T F S S

HONDURAS

La Mesa Intl
62.5nm

Goloson Intl
35.4nm

Night Valley
94.5nm

Nicuragura
118.7nm

On taking off from Guatemala City airport, they headed for La Ceiba on the Caribbean coast of Honduras. Their first error (in hindsight) was that they took off late; the second (in hindsight) is that they headed for a pass to clear the Sierra Madras mountain range in the

hope that the afternoon clouds would clear by the time they got there. They didn't.

The third error (and how could they possibly have known otherwise?) was that they turned right instead of left in their search for an alternative pass. This meant they were left, in Joanna's words,

"heading 30 degrees off-track with a punishing headwind and clouds pinning us to the mountain range, razor sharp peaks below, with absolutely no sign of a pass through and the light rapidly fading. It was a beautiful sunset," she says, finding space for aesthetics in the tension. "But definitely alarming," she adds.

Finally, they were saved from the very real probability of disaster when, at twilight, they spotted a break in the hills and were able to turn G-NUDE north towards the coast and the twinkling lights of La Ceiba's international airfield on the horizon. It was Joanna's first experience of landing a helicopter at night.

"They headed for a pass in the mountains in the hope that the afternoon clouds would clear by the time they got there. They didn't."

"Clouds pinned them to the razor sharp peaks of the mountain range below with absolutely no sign of a pass through and with the light rapidly fading"

FORESTS OF RAIN AND CLOUD

Honduras extends from the Caribbean Sea to the Pacific Ocean. It is a rugged, mountainous country with a fringe of lowland mangroves and savannas along the Caribbean coast. When Christopher Columbus landed in 1506 he named it Honduras - Spanish for 'depths' - because of the deep waters of the Caribbean Sea. But with time to explore the interior, he might easily have named it Bosque de la Montaña after the country's forest-covered mountains, volcanic in origin, which rise to elevations of over 9,000ft and traverse the country in great green ranges, many of them forested to their highest peaks.

Honduras covers an area of more than 43,000 square miles and some four fifths of this territory is mountainous. Though depleted in recent years, some two fifths of the land is still blanketed in trees. Honduras has the most extensive tracts of cloud forest and the largest area of primary forest in Central America - making it a fascinating country to explore on foot, but not the easiest to traverse in a very small helicopter as persistent cloud makes for potentially dangerous flying.

As their name suggests, cloud forests are frequently blanketed in cloud that clings to their canopies almost all year round. Typically cloud forest is a tropical or sub-tropical evergreen mountain forest which can be home to pine and fir trees, giving them the appearance of temperate forests. But generally they flourish at a relatively small band of altitude around 6,000ft, commonly on the saddles of mountains where moisture introduced by settling clouds is more effectively retained.

The persistent mist or cloud at vegetation level at these altitudes results in the reduction of direct sunlight and thus evapotranspiration. The trees in these regions are generally shorter and more heavily stemmed than in forests at lower altitudes. Moisture promotes an abundance of mosses on tree trunks and the forest floor with an abundance of tree ferns and brightly-coloured orchids and bromeliads.

Within cloud forests, much of the precipitation is in the form of fog drip, where the fog condenses on the leaves of the trees and drips onto the rich, peaty ground below. As such, the cloud forests are a source of life for the rest of Honduras, soaking up the water like a vast sponge and releasing it slowly. They are also a rich habitat for an array of exotic birds and animals: the resplendent quetzal, toucans, jays, woodpeckers, solitaires, blue morphos butterflies, cougars, tapirs, sloths and monkeys among them.

In total Honduras boasts almost 40 such cloud forests, the largest of which have been made into national parks; the others are biological reserves or simply water protection areas. For visitors to Honduras prepared to clamber steep slopes to one of the cloud forests, the rewards beneath the forest canopy are an extraordinarily rich biodiversity and crystal clear creeks and waterfalls. To fly above the canopy is another story with the multiple dangers of high altitude, precipitous mountain slopes, unbroken canopies and far from perfect visibility.

"Cloud forests are a source of life for the rest of Honduras, soaking up the water like a vast sponge and releasing it slowly."

NICARAGUA

"This is a country that has atmosphere like no other with its decaying colonial buildings, overwhelming sense of community, and its vibrant street life."

Flying south-west across central Honduras, Joanna and Steve crossed the border into what was already their fifth Central American country as they made their way down the west coast of Nicaragua. This is a region often referred to as a land of lakes and volcanoes and when you examine a map of the terrain they flew over, it is easy to see why.

The impressive line of volcanoes in the Marrabios mountain range, some dormant but others still very much alive, runs from north to south and includes Mombacho just outside Granada and Momotombo near León. Seen from the air, their shapes - some twisted and lop-sided with parts of their cones blown off - betray their violent past, while for others, with serene lakes in what was once the cone, it is their tranquil present that is most striking.

But the experience of Nicaragua that was to linger longest in the memory was meeting the people themselves. While the country's recent history has been a violent one, its sense of community remains defiantly unbowed.

Flight Information

FLIGHT DISTANCE	220NM
FLIGHT TIME	1HR 54MINS

ENTRY:N13° 46.93' W86° 34.19'.   EXIT:N11° 08.28' W85° 43.74'.

HOURS
1h 54m
Nicaragua

TOTAL HOURS FLOWN
OVER NICARAGUA

AVERAGE DIRECTION FLOWN
OVER NICARAGUA

HIGHEST ALTITUDE FLOWN
OVER NICARAGUA

N

Population: Approx. 5,786,000

Area: 50,193 sq miles (129,494 sq km)

Capital City: Managua

Language: Miskito Coastal Creole

Highest Point: Mogoton at 2,438m (7,999ft)

Lowest Point: Pacific Ocean at 0m (0ft)

HONDURAS

NICARAGUA

MANAGUA

Managua
International
Airport

GRANADA

NORTH
PACIFIC
OCEAN

COSTA RICA

CARIBBEAN
SEA

42%

Journey Length

Cumulative Distance: 8,297nm
Cumulative Time: 71hrs 50mins

28°

AVERAGE AIR
TEMPERATURE

Month Two S S M T W T F S S M T W T F S S M T W T F S S M T W T F S S M T W T F S S

Managua Intl
101.2nm

NICARAGUA

Costa Rica
65.5nm

On August 16th, Joanna and Steve were in yet another Central American country, so short is the distance between one and another.

Like a 35mm transparency held to the light, each tiny country is nonetheless dense with colour and definition. One moment they were flying past Masaya, the only volcano on the American continent where a pool of lava constantly simmers and one of the only volcanoes in the world where both walking trails and a vehicle track continue right up to the rim.

The next moment they were strolling through the narrow streets of Granada, Nicaragua's most enchanting of colonial cities. "Come evening we walked to the plaza," says Joanna, "a beautiful place with very old grand buildings that seemed to be slowly disintegrating back to nature. There were tables and chairs and kiosks set up all around, and a big boxing ring commandeering centre stage outside the cathedral. Small groups of people - men, women, children on bikes - gathered to watch young lads fight.

"Then, as the sun set, the street lamps came on and the square was transformed - the boxing ring dismantled and another stage set up for folk dancing. Fantastically talented kids danced salsa and maranga to an applauding crowd. "Then suddenly, across the square, we heard the excited yelps of children. We looked around to see a man with a model of a Spanish bull, laden with Chinese firecrackers, chasing them around.

Smoke and colour everywhere. More men with homemade rockets lit the touch papers and sent them shooting into the sky, before they fell alarmingly into the crowds. Great steaming pots of food and barbeques smouldered as people soaked up the atmosphere. Definitely a fun evening!"

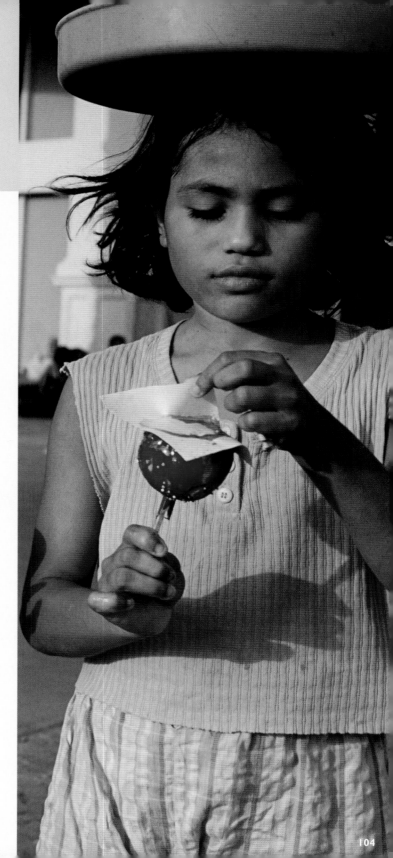

GRANADA

With its colourful colonial neo-classical architecture and cobbled streets, Granada is the most frequently visited city in Nicaragua. Founded by Francisco Hernández de Córdoba in 1524, it is affectionately known as Gran Sultana del Gran Lago, the 'Great Sultan of the Great Lake'. It is at once rich in cultural heritage, politically and economically one of Nicaragua's most vital cities, and also one of its most beautiful located on the shores of the magnificent Lake Cocibolca in the shadow of the Mombacho volcano.

The city's geography has served it well. Through Lake Cocibolca and the San Juan River, it is connected to the Atlantic and during the colonial years maintained a flourishing level of commerce. Nonetheless, it has seen its fair share of scraps and skirmishes. The city has been witness to and victim of many battles with rival English, French and Dutch pirates through the years, and it was also the chosen city of residence for the American filibuster, William Walker, who attempted to take control of Central America as ruling monarch in the mid 1800s.

Fleeing the city after it was eventually surrounded by Guatemalan and Salvadoran troops, one of Walker's generals, Charles Frederick Henningsen, set the city ablaze with the unforgettable words, 'Granada Was Here'. The markings of the fire-torching on the city's cathedrals and historic buildings can still be seen to this day.

The city also had a dispute of a more local kind with rival Nicaraguan city, León. Granada is predominantly Conservative while León is predominantly Liberal, and the two cities' families and political factions squabbled for years in an effort to claim hegemony for their own. In the end a compromise was struck with a third city, Managua, which was granted capital status in 1852.

For the most part Granada avoided damage during the years of conflict in Nicaragua in the 1980s, and today is peaceful, opening its arms to tourists. As is typical of all Central America's colonial cities, Granada is built around its Parque Central, or main square, with cathedral and colonial houses surrounding it. The city boasts a fort, a number of beautiful churches, and a thriving central market selling, amongst the typical fruits and vegetables, freshly caught fish from the lake. It is a city that's best to explore on foot, wandering along its narrow streets and glancing through the doorways of the casonas, the large colonial houses, into the peaceful inner patios filled with tropical plants and rooms furnished with characteristic rocking chairs.

By and large it's an easy going city, where the pleasure is in watching the locals go about their daily business with the ever-present soothing traditional music in the background. But if its drama you're looking for, the best time to visit is August. On the Sunday preceding August 15th there is a major celebration in the form of the Tope de Toro when bulls run free along Granada's streets, tormented by boys running before and alongside them with branches and loud screams. On the Sunday following is the Desfile Hipico, in which the best horses of Nicaragua are paraded along the city's streets - a celebration that draws participants and spectators from across the country.

"The city's geography has served it well. Through Lake Cocibolca and the San Juan River, it is connected to the Atlantic and during the colonial years maintained a flourishing level of trade with the outside world."

Costa Rica

"The people all greet you with the words 'Pura Vida' meaning 'Pure Life to You'. And nothing could be much purer than those epic Pacific beaches and that rocking, rolling surf."

From Nicaragua, Joanna and Steve swooped into Costa Rica, their flight path continuing along the same line of volcanoes they had been flying over further north and which splits the country into two very different, but equally compelling, tropical ecosystems.

Alongside the tropical rainforests of the interior, the country is renowned for its beaches on both the Caribbean and the Pacific coasts as well as its enlightened attitude to conservation which attracts eco-tourists from all over the world. More than a quarter of the country's landmass is protected in one way or another.

Another fascinating aspect of Costa Rica is that it is the only country in the world to have dispensed with its army. This followed the 1948 civil war and has had a number of lasting benefits, not least its reputation as one of the most politically stable countries in Central America. It may also explain the friendliness of its people who call themselves 'Ticos' referring to the frequent use of diminutives in Costa Rican speech.

Flight Information

FLIGHT DISTANCE	289NM
FLIGHT TIME	2HRS 30MINS

ENTRY:N11° 08.28′ W85° 43.74′.   EXIT:N09° 31.36′ W82° 37.89′.

106

TOTAL HOURS FLOWN
OVER COSTA RICA

AVERAGE DIRECTION FLOWN
OVER COSTA RICA

HIGHEST ALTITUDE FLOWN
OVER COSTA RICA

N

NICARAGUA

COSTA RICA

CARIBBEAN
SEA

Daniel Oduber
Quiros International
Airport

SAN JOSE

Tobias
Bolanos International
Airport

Limon

Estrillios

NORTH
PACIFIC
OCEAN

PANAMA

Population: Approx. 4,196,000

Area: 19,730 sq miles (51,100 sq km)

Capital City: San José

Language: Mekatelyu

Highest Point: Cerro Chirripó at 3,810m (12,500ft)

Lowest Point: Pacific Ocean at 0m (0ft)

AVERAGE AIR
TEMPERATURE

43%

Journey Length

Cumulative Distance: 8,587nm
Cumulative Time: 74hrs 20mins

Month Two S S M T W T F S S M T W T F S S M T W T F S S M T W T F S S M T W T F S S

COSTA RICA

Daniel Oduber Quiros Intl
34.4nm

Tobias Bolanos Intl
33.9nm

Panama
35.1nm

Estrillios
89.5nm

Limon
66nm

Steve and Joanna touched down at Liberia international airport in the north west of Costa Rica. The plan was to stay at a pleasing looking 'Auberge du Pelican' that Joanna had researched on the Pacific coast.

But it was Sunday. The flight officials were a little sleepy and declared it only possible to fly to other international airports, nothing as off beat as a small private airstrip aback a B&B. But Joanna and Steve worked their charms. It was their 'luna y miel', their honeymoon, they let drop into conversation. And in moments documents were busily hand-written and stamped and they had flight clearance for the beach.

It wasn't long before they were being greeted by a flurry of children and dogs on the runway, and swimming in the surf on a beach stretching as far as the eye could see. It was a simple but utterly charming Auberge. And they slept soundly that night, until awoken by "a torrential storm, lightning, thunder, wind and rain that could have swept away whole communities," recalls Joanna. "We got up to find our bags floating in water downstairs that was pouring like a torrent through the windows."

A little damp, the next day they made an abortive flight to Costa Rica's capital San Jose, but were pushed back by dense cloud engulfing the hills. So it wasn't until the following morning, in a world transformed and bathed in sunlight, that they finally landed in San Jose and prepared for their next border crossing into Panama.

"It was their 'luna y miel', their honeymoon, they let drop."

COSTA RICA'S 'PURA VIDA'

The Costa Ricans - or Ticos as they're commonly known - have made some unusual choices through the years. Choices that seem to have served them well. Most famously, Costa Rica was the first country in the world to constitutionally abolish its army. And generally it can be said that this small Latin American country with a population of 4.5 million, sandwiched between the Pacific and Caribbean Sea, has enjoyed greater peace and political stability than its neighbours north and south.

But there have been two brief periods that have marred its otherwise democratic development during the 20th century. In 1917-19, Federico Tinoco Granados ruled as a dictator until he was overthrown and forced into exile; and in 1948, a disputed presidential election resulted in a bloody 44-day civil war when 2,000 people died.

It was after this violent upheaval that the military was abolished and a few decades later, as wars and rebellions raged elsewhere in the region during the turbulent 1980s, Costa Rica managed to stay largely neutral. Although not without its problems, it is in part because of its neutrality and in part because of its relative economic stability that the country has been regarded as the Switzerland of Central America.

Another reason, it could also be argued, is because of its mountains. While Switzerland benefits financially from a well-developed and sophisticated ski industry, Costa Rica has very deliberately chosen to focus on another sector of the tourist industry: eco-tourism. The idea behind this relatively new and fast burgeoning sector is to preserve the country's natural resources while also profiting from

the economic opportunity they provide, and few countries can be better placed to do this than Costa Rica.

The country has stunning mountain ranges, active volcanoes and beaches, as well as rivers and streams that attract kayakers and rafters from all over the world. It has a multitude of forests: cloud forest, rain forest, dry forest, transition forest, all within a relatively small region. And crucially, the Costa Rican authorities have ensured that more than 27 per cent of this extraordinary landscape is protected, creating a haven for the country's profusion of flora and fauna, which includes 1,000 species of orchid and 850 species of birds including macaws and toucans with over-sized beaks the colour of mango.

Although small - the country covers just 0.03 per cent of the surface of the globe - it proudly shelters 6 per cent of the planet's biodiversity and nature lovers want to enjoy it in increasing numbers. Tourism now earns more foreign exchange than the country's former staple exports, bananas and coffee, combined. It isn't easy to maintain the delicate balance between preserving natural resources and making money from them, but generally Ticos are proud of their natural heritage and recognise that the twin goals of environmental conservation and economic prosperity aren't necessarily mutually exclusive.

The government has also now stated that it wants Costa Rica to be the first country to become carbon neutral, and to achieve this by 2021. Currently, annual carbon dioxide emissions per person in Costa Rica are 1.2 metric tons, compared with 19.9 metric tons in the United States. It is a goal that might just be within its reach.

"In Costa Rica, numbers tell a story. Although tiny, it accounts for six per cent of the world's entire biodiversity and is home to 1,000 species of orchids and 850 species of birds including macaws and toucans with over-sized beaks the colour of mango."

PANAMA

"Panama is an amazing mix of Western and tribal cultures. I just wanted to lose myself with my camera and soak it all up."

Panama, famous the world over for both its distinctive hats and its canal linking the Atlantic with the Pacific Ocean, is a narrow isthmus of land that twists and curves back on itself from the Costa Rican border in the north to the infamous Darien Gap and the border with Colombia in the south.

And for Joanna, whose burgeoning interest in indigenous cultures was later to lead her to study social anthropology, by far the most compelling aspect of the country were the inhabitants of the San Blas Islands, part of an archipelago off the north coast. The Kuna people are renowned for their colourful handicrafts, in particular the decorative 'molas' which the women wear on the front and back of their blouses.

Staying on tiny Sapibenega Island, Joanna and Steve took a boat to neighbouring Ukupseni, home to a community of 3,000 Kuna. It was to turn out to be one of the most memorable excursions of their trip.

Flight Information

| FLIGHT DISTANCE | 401NM |
| FLIGHT TIME | 3HRS 28MINS |

ENTRY: N09° 31.36′ W82° 37.89′.   EXIT: N08° 34.83′ W77° 24.43′.

112

HOURS
3h 28m
Panama

TOTAL HOURS FLOWN
OVER PANAMA

N

AVERAGE DIRECTION FLOWN
OVER PANAMA

HIGHEST ALTITUDE FLOWN
OVER PANAMA

2.7°
AVERAGE AIR
TEMPERATURE

45%

Journey Length

Cumulative Distance: 8,988nm
Cumulative Time: 77hrs 48mins

DARIEN GAP

COLOMBIA

Manuel Nino International Airport

Bocas del
Toro International Airport

COSTA
RICA

PANAMA

CARIBBEAN
SEA

Coast Route

San Blas Islands

Portobello
Beach House

Panama Canal

PANAMA CITY

Marcos A Gelabert
International Airport

NORTH
PACIFIC
OCEAN

Population: Approx. 3,310,000

Area: 29,157 sq miles (75,517 sq km)

Capital City: Panama City

Language: Spanish

Highest Point: Volcan de Chiriqui at 3,475m (11,401ft)

Lowest Point: Pacific Ocean at 0m (0ft)

Month Two S S M T W T F S S M T W T F S S M T W T F S S M T W T F S S M T W T F S S

Manuel
Nino Intl
7.9nm

Survivor Island
6.2nm

Panama Canal
82.5nm

Portabello
35nm

San Blas Islands
55.6nm

Columbia
129.6nm

PANAMA

Bocas Del
Toro Intl
17.1nm

Coast Route
67.2nm

Marcos A Gelabert Intl
33.8nm

Beach House
5.4nm

Marcos A Gelabert Intl
55.8nm

"Of the 365 islands and islets that make up the archipelago - some no more than a disc of sand with a single palm tree - only 50 are inhabited."

They were soon flying across the border into Panama, landing briefly at Changuinola, before opening the throttle and sweeping along the Archipelago de Bocas del Toro. Then it was on again skimming the length of a beautiful, straight, expansive stretch of beach, 20ft off the ground at 112mph. "It was like the opening scene of a Discovery Channel series," says Steve.

At the port town of Colón, on Panama's Caribbean coast, they flew over the mouth of the country's famous Panama Canal where container ships waited in turn to funnel through a bottleneck of lochs into Lake Gatun and the canal itself. This links the Caribbean and Atlantic Ocean to the Pacific, a distance of just 36 miles. Joanna and Steve flew it in 20 minutes.

At the Pacific end in Panama City, the country's capital, they parked G-NUDE at the region's main authorised Robinson dealership, Helipan. News of their travels preceded them. Thomas Exenberger, founder of Helipan, had spotted a small article about Steve's and Q's Arctic exploits in the back of the Robinson monthly circular, and couldn't do enough to help them.

"He organised taxis and tours for us in this mad, bustling city," says Joanna. "It's an amazing place, with a busy skyline of offices, apartments and hotels rubbing along next to shanty towns. We found a fabulous Japanese restaurant and popped into a supermarket for a few provisions. But we couldn't help noticing the guards, armed with pump action shotguns."

Thomas had other surprises in store as well. He owned a beach house at Portobello, east of Colón, and with the sort of hospitality almost expected of fellow pilots by this stage of the journey, he offered Joanna and Steve the keys. So they happily stopped off here before flying east again to the Archipelago de San Blas, home of the Kuna - a Panamanian tribe numbering some 35,000.

Of the 365 islands and islets that make up the archipelago - some

no more than a disc of sand with a single palm tree - only 50 are inhabited. Joanna and Steve stayed at Sapibenega Island, a verdant jewel with palm trees and white sand beach small enough for the average swimmer to circumnavigate. Once deserted, it had been developed by Paliwitus, a local Kuna man, who had built a scattering of simple huts around its perimeter with a bar, so creating a small hotel in paradise.

A short boat ride took Joanna and Steve to the island of Ukupseni, also called Playón Chico, one of the most populous islands of the archipelago. Staggeringly 3,000 people live on this strip of land - only 300 yards by 400 yards in size and just a foot above the lapping waves - and about two thirds of them are children. They are a sociable people and at the time Joanna and Steve visited, they were preparing for an inauguration fiesta to celebrate the completion of a new bridge spanning the 200 yards of water between the island and the mainland.

"We walked around the small town and the narrow streets in amazement," says Joanna. "Each family has a thatched hut for cooking and one for sleeping, all built in a ramshackle manner on any space available. The streets were just swaying with people dressed in a mix of jeans and T-shirts and beautiful traditional dress, dancing and playing music and games, flags flying everywhere."

Confessing that she wished she had studied anthropology before rather than after their journey, they were then shown 'the congress house'. "It was a large hut in the centre of the island where only men did business," Joanna recalls. "There were four hammocks in the middle under a shelf with portraits and an antique clock, where the chiefs, tiny in stature, lay chattering while others relaxed on benches around the perimeter and scribes recorded their words."

Joanna was later to learn that the Kuna has the most advanced political system of any tribal group in Latin America.

"The women, more than the men, stick to traditional dress: wrap around skirts, and beautifully hand-stitched blouses, called Molas, which they make from several layers of elaborately embroidered panels."

THE KUNA

The Kuna is a strongly-knit traditional society of Native Americans with a population of 53,000 or so, the majority of whom live on a string of tropical islands surrounded by crystal waters and coral reef called the San Blas Archipelago, stretched along Panama's Caribbean coast. There are also Kuna people who live in scattered settlements in the Darien Province of Panama and in Colombia, and a few who have migrated to the cities.

For the main, though, they live in three semi-autonomous reservations, or comarca, granted to them following a rebellion against government policies banning traditional dress and religious customs, in 1925 - and of these, by far the largest is Kuna Yala, encompassing the 365 islands of the San Blas Archipelago. Here, geographically detached from the mainland, they have, with the notable exception of tourism, largely resisted assimilating Western culture and maintained their traditional lifestyle.

On the islands, the Kuna people speak their own language, Tule. They live in thatched huts made from materials readily found in the forest; and the women, more than the men, stick to traditional dress: wrap around skirts, and beautifully hand-stitched blouses, called Molas, which they make from several layers of elaborately embroidered panels.

Kuna families are matrilineal; a young man, after marriage, lives in his mother-in-law's house and works under apprenticeship to his father-in-law, with the division of labour along traditional lines: the women preparing food, collecting water, unloading the boats, washing, cleaning; while the men cultivate the land, gather firewood,

repair the house, weave baskets and carve wooden utensils. The exception to this being albino men, of which there are an unusually large number among the Kuna people, who assume duties traditionally assigned to women, including the making of molas. In Kuna mythology, albinos are regarded as a special race. Only they can defend the moon against a dragon that on rare occasions tries to eat it; only they are allowed out on the night of an eclipse.

Their political life is one of the most advanced of any tribal group in Latin America. Each community has its own congress led by a Sohila, or chief, who is both political and spiritual leader, and chants songs relating to the history, legends and laws of the Kuna, as well as administering day-to-day political and social affairs. The Onmaket Nega, or congress house, often a simple thatched hut with earthen floor, is the centre of all such activity. Here men, women and children gather to listen to the Sohila chant, reinforcing their cultural moral code; and here, too, formal gatherings of the eldest men are held, to discuss laws and settle disputes.

Though far from perfect, their self-governance has gone a long way to help protect their traditional culture from the most significant threat of modern life: tourism. Mistakes have been made; inevitably a number of young Kuna men favour cash from tourists over the tribe's traditional, collectively-owned agriculture. But, accepting they cannot be entirely immune from the impact of tourism, they have nonetheless enforced a few self-guarding rules to ensure the benefits outweigh the drawbacks as far as it's possible. Outsiders are not allowed to own land, and only eco-tourism and cultural heritage tourism are permitted.

"Geographically detached from the mainland, the Kuna have largely resisted being assimilated by Western culture and have maintained their traditional lifestyle."

SOUTH AMERICA

Fast approaching the equator and the mid-point in their journey, some serious challenges now awaited the two pilots. The massive scale of the Amazon rainforest was a daunting prospect. So too some of the increasingly bureaucratic airport regulations. But their goal was in sight and the adventure in full swing.

COLOMBIA ▶ VENEZUELA ▶ BRAZIL ▶ PERU ▶ ARGENTINA ▶ CHILE

COLOMBIA

"While a city like Cartagena may be a Spanish colonial masterpiece, Colombia is not the place for engine failure in guerrilla infested territory."

After crossing the lawless and infamous Darien Gap to the north, Joanna's and Steve's first contact with South America proper was the beautiful town of Cartagena, a Spanish colonial gem which was once famously stormed by the English 'pirate', Sir Francis Drake.

Although renowned and feared for kidnapping and political volatility, Colombia is for the most part one of the most cultured countries in South America. Cartagena has featured in many of the books of one-time resident, Gabriel García Marquez, and the cobbled streets, colonial houses with their trademark courtyards, fruit-sellers and street-corner musicians, are a far cry from Colombia's traditional violent image.

Nonetheless, it was with some trepidation that they headed out towards the Sierra Nevada mountains to the east which rise to more than 18,500ft within just a few miles of the coast. The mountains are the home of the famously reclusive Kogi Indians who are one of the few tribal peoples to have successfully retained their cultural and spiritual rituals and beliefs since before the Spanish conquest.

Flight Information

FLIGHT DISTANCE	300NM
FLIGHT TIME	2HRS 36MINS

ENTRY:N08° 34.83' W77° 24.43'.   EXIT:N10° 32.81' W72° 48.76'.

124

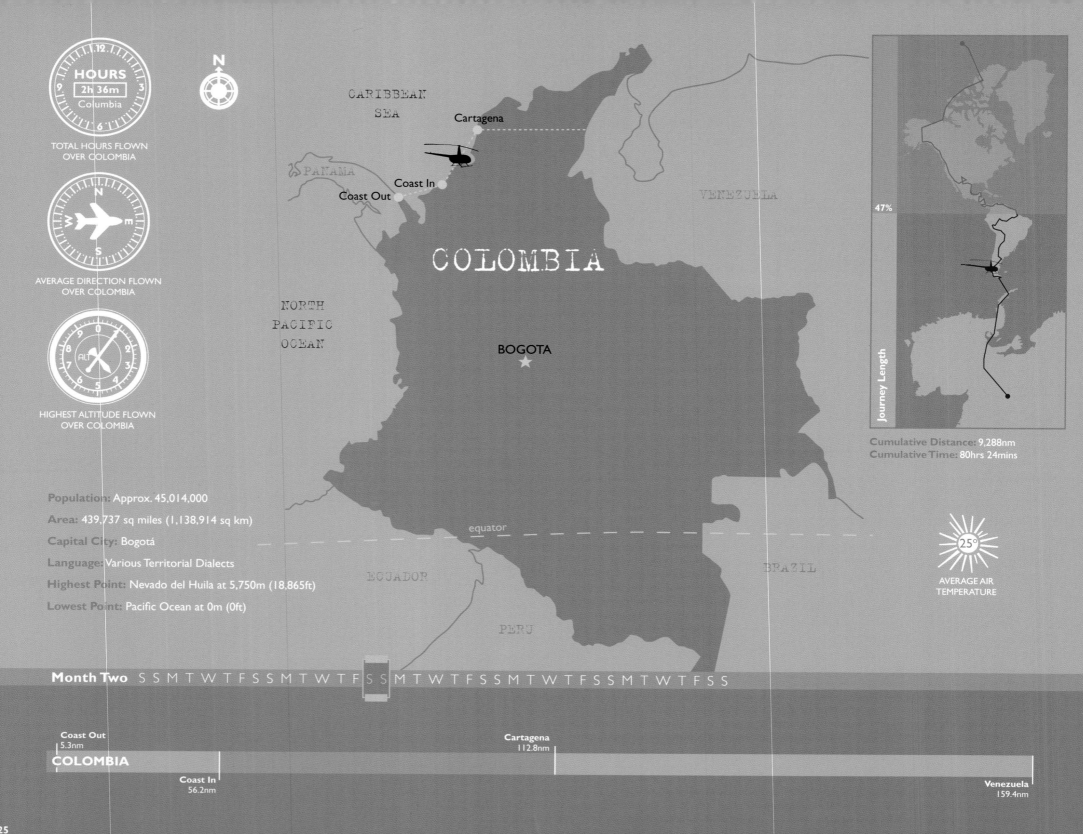

HOURS
2h 36m
Columbia

TOTAL HOURS FLOWN
OVER COLOMBIA

AVERAGE DIRECTION FLOWN
OVER COLOMBIA

ALT

HIGHEST ALTITUDE FLOWN
OVER COLOMBIA

N

CARIBBEAN
SEA

Cartagena

PANAMA

Coast In

Coast Out

COLOMBIA

NORTH
PACIFIC
OCEAN

BOGOTA

VENEZUELA

47%

Journey Length

Cumulative Distance: 9,288nm
Cumulative Time: 80hrs 24mins

Population: Approx. 45,014,000

Area: 439,737 sq miles (1,138,914 sq km)

Capital City: Bogotá

Language: Various Territorial Dialects

Highest Point: Nevado del Huila at 5,750m (18,865ft)

Lowest Point: Pacific Ocean at 0m (0ft)

equator

25°

AVERAGE AIR
TEMPERATURE

ECUADOR

BRAZIL

PERU

Month Two S S M T W T F S S M T W T F S S M T W T F S S M T W T F S S M T W T F S S

Coast Out
5.3nm

Cartagena
112.8nm

COLOMBIA

Coast In
56.2nm

Venezuela
159.4nm

"A strikingly beautiful and safe city with Spanish colonial buildings, city walls and fortresses."

GUERRERO

3971

Diary

If Joanna's and Steve's trip had been solely about setting records, flying from the northern to the southern tip of the Americas in the fastest possible time, the obvious line from Panama would have been directly south through Colombia, Peru, Chile, maybe taking in Argentina.

But it wasn't. One thing that Steve had long wished to experience was to fly the length of the Amazon, which meant their taking a broad sweep east along the northern coast of South America - before dipping south into Brazil and taking a huge hairpin turn back west, along this most massive of rivers in the world. Alone, Joanna might have by-passed the Amazon. She had spent time there before; and interestingly, in the first mention of any concerns her family might have expressed about her safety, Joanna confessed that flying over the Amazon basin was the one leg of the journey that her father had been truly worried about. As a young man straight from school, Joanna's father, Sir Paul Vestey, had served his apprenticeship in the family business packing meat in one of its factories in Argentina, and had seen the dense canopy of the Amazonian forest with his own eyes. Unquestionably there were risks involved in flying a single-engine helicopter over such unforgiving terrain, but first they had to get there. Their first step was across the border from Panama City to Cartagena de Indias, a large city seaport with a beautiful colonial old quarter on the northern coast of Colombia. By road, this journey is impossible. A traveller on foot with laden donkey might succeed, but would have to pass through the infamous Darien Gap between Central and South America, with its swamps and dense forest and reputation for drug runners, kidnappings and lawlessness. No tarmac is laid.

Joanna and Steve had to pick a line between flying over this and the open Caribbean Sea, again a disquieting option, considering their decision to abandon the precautionary measure of fixing sea floats in order to gain sufficient range. But all went well. G-NUDE flew like a dream, and on the afternoon of August 25th, 2002, before any threatening

126

cumulonimbus clouds had time to build up, Joanna and Steve safely touched down in Cartagena on Colombia's Caribbean coast.

In a country notorious for its political unrest, kidnappings, and illicit drug trafficking, they assumed that Cartagena - the capital of Bolíva Department with a population upwards of a million- would be a place to be extra vigilant. They need not have worried. This strikingly beautiful city with its Spanish colonial walls and fortresses, designated a UNESCO World Heritage Site in 1984, was a delight. "We felt completely at ease even after night fell," says Joanna. "There were people dancing in the plazas; it's a really friendly place."

It wasn't until the following morning that their nerves were pricked. Their plan had been to fly across the border to Maracaibo in Venezuela, but their preferred route along the coast, as it turned out, was a restricted area. Joanna, having failed after repeated efforts to procure aviation maps for South America, proffered her newly-acquired road map to the airport officials to suggest an alternative route, and had it returned, dotted with the letter 'G' in circles.

"What do they mean?" quizzed Steve. "Guerrillas," said Joanna. "To be avoided." People seemed keen to remind them of the potential dangers. A Canadian helicopter had recently been hijacked and a light aircraft shot down. Ironically, there was also a risk of being shot down by the authorities, the reason being that a legitimate pilot was supposedly allocated a password as proof that he or she was not a drug trafficker. Yet nobody seemed to know what these passwords were.

To add to this, they had to fly over an 11,000ft mountain range in threatening weather with towering cumulonimbus forecast and in a helicopter that was revealing signs of having had a very, very long journey. G-NUDE was sounding as if she might be firing short of a cylinder.

THE KOGI

The Sierra Nevada de Santa Marta is an isolated mountain massif with snow-capped peaks that soar more than 18,500ft above the sun-soaked Caribbean coast of Colombia, the highest coastal massif in the world. For the Kogi - descendents of the ancient Tayrona civilization - who today number as few as 12,000 people, it is also home.

For half a millennium since the Spanish conquest, when they fled almost certain death and pestilence by retreating to the forested slopes of the mountains, the Kogi have regarded the Sierra Nevada de Santa Marta to be sacred, the heart of the world. Their mission, they believe, is to be custodian both to it, and in turn, the planet.

The Kogi live in the higher regions of the Sierra Nevada. They plant crops and live off the land, moving from place to place, from one village of simple thatched abodes to another, to meet their nutritional needs without putting strain on the environment. They are also reclusive, preferring not to mix with outsiders.

To this day, they remain true to their ancient laws - the moral, ecological, and spiritual dictates of a creator they identify as the Mother - and are still led and inspired by a ritual priesthood. The priests, or Mamas, are chosen from birth and spend the first nine years of their childhood in total darkness learning the ancient secrets of the spiritual world.

When the Mamas speak, they immediately reveal their reference points as far removed from those of the Western world.

They talk of Se, the spiritual core of all existence; and Aluna, human thought, soul, and imagination. To the Kogi, it isn't what is seen and measurable that is important as much as what exists in the many realms of meanings and connections that lie beneath the tangible realities of the world.

Nine is an important number for them: the nine-layered universe of their cosmology; the nine-tiered temple in which they gather; the nine months a child spends in its mother's womb. Each reflect and inform the other. A hill can also be a house; the mountains a model of the universe; the hairs on a person's body echo the trees on the mountain slopes. Every element of nature is imbued with higher significance and every feature of the world mirrors the whole.

Which is why the recent ecological changes they have seen in their own environment, from the melting snows on the mountain tops to the reduced flow of the rivers, caused them in 1988 to break their silence and send a message to the rest of the world. If their mountains were ill, they reasoned, then the whole world must be in trouble.

The resulting film 'From the Heart of the World', a BBC documentary made by Director, Alan Ereira, is a heart-felt warning from the Kogi, the 'Elder Brother', to us, the wayward 'Younger Brother'. Its message? That unless we learn quickly to change our ways and respect the Mother that feeds and nurtures us, then the planet and all the creatures that are dependent upon it, including ourselves, are in imminent and mortal danger.

"To the Kogi, it isn't what is seen and measurable that is important so much as what exists in the many realms of meanings and connections that lie beneath the tangible realities of the world."

VENEZUELA

"If dinosaurs still roamed the Earth, this is where you'd find them. The tepuis - table-top mountains - are quite phenomenal."

Of all the incredible landscapes Joanna and Steve flew over during the course of their epic journey, few came close to the extraordinary table-top mountains, known as tepuis, which are characteristic of the Gran Sabana region in the south of the country.

First explored by Westerners during the Victorian era, they were the setting for Sir Arthur Conan Doyle's book The Lost World, and his imaginary Jurassic inhabitants were hard to banish from the mind as they flew overhead.

The tepuis are made of sedimentary sandstone which was once the sea-bed and date back to a time when South America and Africa were joined. The most famous tepuis are Mt. Roraima in Canaima National Park and Auyan Tepui, source of the highest waterfall in the world. And it was on the latter that the Canadian gold-prospector and adventurer, Jimmy Angel, crash-landed his Flamingo monoplane in 1937, thereby discovering the falls to which he later gave his name.

Flight Information

FLIGHT DISTANCE	1,786NM
FLIGHT TIME	15HRS 28MINS

ENTRY:N10° 32.81′ W72° 48.76′.   EXIT:N03° 32.05′ W52° 03.69′.

130

HOURS
15h 28m
Venezuela

TOTAL HOURS FLOWN
OVER VENEZUELA

N

AVERAGE DIRECTION FLOWN
OVER VENEZUELA

HIGHEST ALTITUDE FLOWN
OVER VENEZUELA

CARIBBEAN
SEA

La Chinita International
Airport

CARACAS

Sinamaica

El Avilla

Simon
Bolivar International
Airport

LAKE MARACAIBO

VENEZUELA

Manuel
Carlos Piar

Cheddi
Jagan International
Airport

Angel Falls

Journey Length

55%

COLOMBIA

CANAIMA NATIONAL PARK

Cumulative Distance: 11,074nm
Cumulative Time: 95hrs 52mins

SURINAM

Population: Approx. 26,415,000

Area: 352,140 sq miles (912,050 sq km)

Capital City: Caracas

Language: Spanish

Highest Point: Pico Bolivar (La Columna) at 5,007m (16,427ft)

Lowest Point: Caribbean Sea at 0m (0ft)

GUYANA

BRAZIL

29°

AVERAGE AIR
TEMPERATURE

Month Two S S M T W T F S S M T W T F S S M T W T F S S M T W T F S S M T W T F S S

La Chinita Intl
64.1nm

Simon Bolivar Intl
291.2nm

VENEZUELA

Sinamaica
25.6nm

Manuel Carlos Piar
55.8nm

nother tense flight followed as they flew east from Colombia. They touched down at Maracaibo, relieved, and acutely aware that their first priority was a service for G-NUDE. Next stop, El Avila, a heliport just south of Caracas. "It was mad," says

Joanna, "sky machines like you've never seen, tucked into a beautifully designed three-storey hangar, virtually hidden in a valley, mountains all around; very James Bond."

Steve walked into the hanger. "Hello," he said, "we've just flown from the North Pole, any chance

of a service?" Within minutes Nudie was in the hangar alongside the most enormous collection of pristine helicopters.

"Six people set about stripping everything down and checking everything in the minutest detail," recalls Joanna. "They replaced our missing strobe bulb and checked

the plugs, belts and so on. Everything was hosed down and four people set about polishing and vacuuming every available bit of surface. When we enquired about the cost, Carlos, the man in charge, just smiled and said it was a honeymoon gift - extraordinary generosity from people we had just met."

They were to see another side of Venezuelan life, though, when the team from El Avila escorted them to a small, single-roomed clinic in the middle of a vast shanty town sprawling across the hills surrounding Caracas to get their yellow fever jabs, essential for their onward journey to Brazil.

"There were tens of thousands of people living in breeze block and corrugated iron dwellings, perched precariously on impossibly steep hillsides," says Joanna, "a very sad sight given the millions of pounds worth of flying machines we'd just seen."

Acutely aware, and appreciative, of the extraordinary privilege she and Steve shared in their flight of freedom across the Americas, it might seem churlish to highlight inconveniences that curtailed their keenly sought independence: rigid flight plans, bureaucratic customs officials, the weather. But if ever such frustrations clouded the spirit and wonder of their adventure, there was one experience that they were about to share from which they could only conclude that a single helicopter flight can transcend virtually any experience on Earth.

Francisco Pacheco, owner of El Avila, was himself a record-breaking helicopter pilot, who in 1992, with co-pilot Tomas Spanier, had flown from Venezuela to Spain - the longest ever trans-ocean flight. He offered them a spin in his MD 500D, the very same machine in which he had crossed the Atlantic.

their journey to Canaima National Park, famous for its tepuis - or table-top mountains - in the south and east of the country.

They landed that evening at a small helipad - one that Francisco had had built - at a lodge in the rainforest, by a lagoon into which no fewer than seven waterfalls cascaded. The following day, August 30th, 2002, was Joanna's 30th birthday. Difficult to imagine a more beautiful place to awake in celebration.

That morning they had hoped to fly to Angel Falls, at 3,287ft the highest waterfall in the world. They had planned to reach it early before the tourist rush, but were beaten back by the weather. An hour or so passed and they tried again, edging their way in cloud around the steep cliffs of a vast tepuis before Steve spotted, just off-course, a window of light and headed for it. "It was like

"Edging their way in cloud around the vast tepuis, Steve spotted a window of light. 'It was like smashing through a glass pane into a cathedral. A vaulted ceiling of cloud overhead; massive, walls on either side; and light streaming in.'"

"It was more like a dance than flying," says Joanna, "the experience was so overwhelming that I sat with tears streaming down my face. We climbed vertically before spinning, twisting and rushing towards the ground, pulling out of the dive just short of the trees and flying through the hills to a waterfall. Then, suddenly, we were spiralling down, down into a tiny, narrow canyon carved into the hills. Could I have done this? Never! The rotor blades sliced through the spray, rainbows everywhere."

Joanna and Steve bid an emotional farewell to Francisco and his team, sorry to be leaving and swearing that, one day, they'd return to learn to fly a MD 500D, the Ferrari of the helicopter world. Meanwhile they were very grateful that G-NUDE was flying just perfectly after her service, all set for the next leg of

smashing through a glass pane into a cathedral," says Steve, "a vaulted ceiling of cloud overhead, massive, granite walls of the tepuis either side, and light streaming in from the far end."

They landed, close to a canyon at Kavac, and befriending a local man, followed him and his children on foot, "up and up, twisting, winding our way along an ever-narrowing path," says Joanna, "to an exquisite waterfall, steep canyon walls and pools of copper-coloured water, a slice of heaven where the local townspeople collect their water."

The afternoon brought sunshine, and the pair were able to fly to Angel Falls after all. Peering down from their elevated eagle's eye, they could just spot the tiny river tributaries that the tourist boats had negotiated earlier the same day.

JOURNEY TO THE LOST WORLD

Often called the Lost World, after Arthur Conan Doyle's fantasy novel set on a plateau inhabited by dinosaurs and ape-like men, Venezuela's tepuis - in fact as well as fiction - are flat-topped table mountains that rise sheer out of the forest and savanna in the remote south of the country.

Mt. Roraima, an account of whose discovery inspired Conan Doyle's novel, towers more than 2,000ft above the plains below and is the highest tepui in the region. Reports of the existence of these pre-historic worlds by the explorer Robert Schomburgk during the Victorian era coincided with the first flush of dinosaur mania. Conan Doyle's epic tale stoked the public imagination still further.

Formed by the erosion of sea-bed sediment when the African and South American continents drifted apart, they are among the world's oldest geological formations dating back to the pre-cambrian era some two billion years ago. One third of the plants found in the park are found nowhere else on the planet. Over the aeons the summits of the tepuis, sometimes dubbed the Galapagos of the Skies, have evolved their own unique ecosystems and as many as 50 per cent of the species that live on them are found nowhere else on the planet.

Tepui is the name given to these mountains by the indigenous Pemón Indians of Venezuela's Gran Sabana. It literally means 'house of the gods' and there are more than 100 of them in the region. For the Pemóns, the whole landscape is represented in their myths

and legends with the mountains, waterfalls and rivers all serving as reminders of the origins of their world.

To the Pemón Indians, Mt Roraima has special significance. They see it as the stump of a mighty tree that once held all the fruits and tuberous vegetables in the world, until it was felled by one of their ancestors, crashing to the ground and unleashing a terrible flood. 'Roroi' means 'blue-green'; and 'ma' means 'great'. On Roraima's plateau lies the triple border point of Venezuela, Guyana and Brazil; and the Pemóns refer to it also as 'The Mother of all Waters' as it feeds the three major river systems of the three countries respectively: namely the Orinoco, the Essequibo, and the Amazon itself.

The tepuis lie in what is now Venezuela's vast Canaima National Park. At more than 11,500 square miles, the park is the size of Belgium, and in 1994 was granted World Heritage Status in recognition of its extraordinary scenery, together with its geological and biological importance.

The park is also home to what is frequently considered the eighth wonder of the world: Angel Falls. At 3,287ft, and with a clear drop of 2,684ft, Angel Falls is nearly eight times higher than Victoria Falls and sixteen times higher than Niagara Falls. And it was on Auyan Tepui, from which they plunge, that the Canadian gold-prospector and adventurer Jimmy Angel crash-landed his Flamingo monoplane in 1937, thereby discovering the falls to which he later gave his name.

"Over the aeons the summits of the tepuis, sometimes dubbed the Galapagos of the Skies, have evolved their own unique ecosystems and as many as 50 per cent of the species that live on them are found nowhere else on the planet."

BRAZIL

"It's actually far more dangerous flying over the Amazon than the Poles. At least at the Poles you can touch down on ice. Here the trees would just swallow you up."

Fast approaching the equator and the half-way point in their journey, this was the moment when both Joanna and Steve both felt that their ambition to fly the length of the Americas was really within their grasp. But one of their greatest challenges still awaited them in the form of the world's largest river, the Amazon.

The surrounding river basin is home to more than half the planet's remaining rainforest and while they had already flown over extensive areas of dense jungle, none even remotely compared to the vast scale of the Amazon. While there is some debate whether or not it is the longest river in the world - some (mostly Egyptians!) claim that distinction for the Nile - it is certainly the most intimidating to navigate either on the ground or in the air.

With huge swathes of the forest beneath them uncharted, and equipped only with a very large scale road map, their only realistic means of navigation was to follow the sinuous path of the river itself.

Flight Information

FLIGHT DISTANCE	1,563NM
FLIGHT TIME	13HRS 31MINS

ENTRY: N03° 32.05' W52° 03.69'.   EXIT: S04° 06.39' W70° 00.50'.

HOURS
13h 31m
Brazil

TOTAL HOURS FLOWN
OVER BRAZIL

AVERAGE DIRECTION FLOWN
OVER BRAZIL

HIGHEST ALTITUDE FLOWN
OVER BRAZIL

Population: Approx. 26,415,000

Area: 3,287,612 sq miles (8,514,877 sq km)

Capital City: Brasília

Language: Portuguese

Highest Point: Pico da Neblina at 3,014m (9,888ft)

Lowest Point: Atlantic Ocean at 0m (0ft)

VENEZUELA
GUYANA
SURINAM
COLOMBIA

equator

Macapa International Airport

Amazon 1

Amazon 3

MANUAS

Santarem

Tabatinga
International
Airport

Tefe

Amazon 2

Ponta Pelada International
Airport

SOUTH
PACIFIC OCEAN

PERU

BOLIVIA

BRAZIL

BRASÍLIA

SOUTH
ATLANTIC
OCEAN

CHILE

RIO DE JANEIRO

SAN PAULO

ARGENTINA

URUGUAY

63%

Journey Length

Cumulative Distance: 12,637nm
Cumulative Time: 109hrs 23mins

28°

AVERAGE AIR
TEMPERATURE

Month Two S S M T W T F S S M T W T F S S M T W T F S S M T W T F S S M T W T F S S

Macapa Intl 217.3nm		Amazon 1 68.6nm		Amazon 2 134.1nm		Amazon 3 127.4nm	Alfredo Vasquez Cobo 3.5nm

BRAZIL

Santarem Intl 267.8nm · Ponta Pelada 257.5nm · Tefe 165.5nm · Tabatinga Intl 242nm · Peru 6.5nm

'The 'meeting of the waters', the confluence of the Rivers Negro and Amazon with their contrasting dark and clear waters running alongside each other like the stripes in a tube of toothpaste."

Diary

Rested now and impatient to fly the length of the Amazon, Steve and Joanna sped through Guyana, Suriname, and French Guiana crossing the border into Brazil, landing at Macapá, a mining city at the mouth of the great Amazon River, on 1st September. In distance, this marked the exact half-way spot of Steve's journey from North to South Pole: Macapá lies on the equator.

"We were really settling into the journey by this stage," says Steve, "feeling at one with the machine. We'd lost that anxiety of inexperience and were taking on new challenges in our stride. We were daring to dream."

It was a sentiment Joanna endorsed. "At the start I had said, let's just see how far we get, but by this stage I felt, yes, we can do this; we can fly to Chile."

It was as well, for the challenge they were about to undertake was the greatest yet. On their journey from Venezuela, they had already flown over extensive areas of rainforest, but none quite as vast as that of the Amazon. The Amazon contains more than half of the planet's remaining forest. "The canopies are massive," says Joanna, "it's far more dangerous than flying in the Arctic or Antarctic. At least there you can touch down on the ice; here the trees would just swallow you up."

Their first day's flight, deep into the interior, was thankfully uneventful. They refuelled at Santerem, continuing their journey deeper still into the interior, to Manaus. It was a long day, 600 miles over tree tops. This far from the Atlantic Ocean and, staggeringly, Manaus is still a port.

The Pan American highway runs north to south through the city which is also a hub for tourists who have travelled across continents to see the 'meeting of the waters', the confluence of the Rivers Negro and Amazon with their contrasting dark and clear waters running alongside each other like the stripes in a tube of toothpaste.

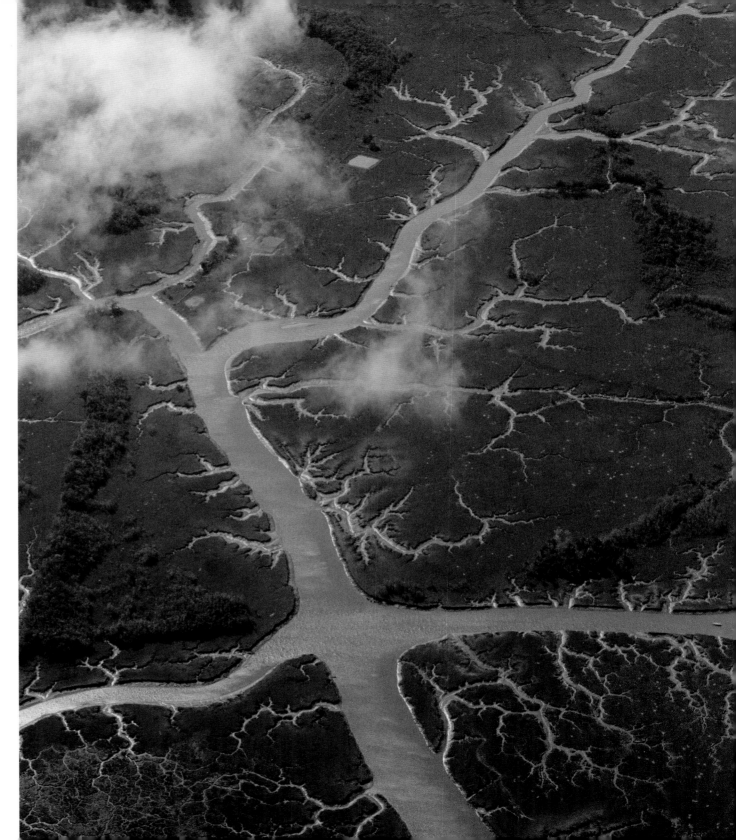

They landed G-NUDE on the helipad of Ariau Amazon Towers, a fanciful, lofty hotel built among the tree tops with restaurants, shops, pools and cyber cafes, interlinked with a cobweb of catwalks. It was here that a fierce, frighteningly large monkey scrambled over Joanna and Steve onto the backseat of the helicopter, and ate its way through a tube of Pringles.

Here they rested for a couple of days, before girding their loins for the next stage of the journey, west again along the Amazon. There was a local pilot staying at the hotel. He could shed no light on the territory over which they were about to fly, other than to remind them of a missionary family who had taken a similar flight line not so long ago, and been shot down by a Peruvian air force pilot who mistook their Cessna seaplane for a drug-smuggling plane, with tragic results.

A great deal of the forest remains uncharted. Virtually no markings appear on the GPS, and equipped only with a very large scale road map, their only practical means of navigation was to follow the Amazon itself, and hope that at one of its numerous confluences, they didn't turn left instead of right, or right instead of left, and end up a tributary with a falling fuel gauge and no place to land.

These concerns weighed heavily on their minds as Steve fired the ignition, immediately to be alerted to the faltering sound of a failed spark plug. It was a moment when Joanna was happier than usual to have a husband who was an engineer with a bag of tools at hand. Normally, they might have resolved the problem and test flown G-NUDE in the knowledge they could land if the problem persisted.

But here the nearest landing point was 20 minutes away in Manaus, or else a tight U-turn to a very small landing pad in the trees. Steve tested one cylinder, then another in turn, replaced the offending sparkplug, and gingerly lifted G-NUDE off the helipad, over the trees and away. "The view from the air was amazing," says Joanna, ever sanguine. "It looked as though there were green landing spaces all around the trees, until we got close and realised they were mattresses of floating weed - a sure casket for Nudie had we landed in it."

Another 300 miles over the forest and they touched down to refuel at Tefe, before flying on again to Tabatinga, still in Brazil. Then it was on again, just a hop over the border, to Leticia in Colombia. Together with Santa Rosa in Peru, this Tres Fronteras urbanisation stretching along the shores of the Amazon, is home to more than 100,000 residents. It was the largest conurbation Joanna and Steve would see until they landed at their next destination, Iquitos in Peru.

"The Amazon is far more dangerous than flying in either the Arctic or Antarctic. "At least there you can touch down on the ice," says Joanna. "Here the trees would just swallow you up."

"We'd lost that anxiety of inexperience and were
taking on new challenges in our stride. We were

AMAZON ODYSSEY

The Nile and the Amazon have long competed for the title of the longest river in the world with most agreeing that the Nile is fractionally longer. But there is no argument over which is greatest in terms of sheer scale: no other river comes close to the Amazon. The Amazon is the most voluminous river on Earth. In total it is made up of over 1,000 tributaries - many of which are more than 1,000 miles long - and drains 2,727,000 square miles, roughly 40 per cent of South America, an area equivalent to the size of the U.S.

This, together with the sheer volume of rain in the equatorial zone in which it lies (over 400 inches a year), means that it carries an enormous quantity of fresh water, albeit thick with sediment, to the open sea. This accounts for around 20 per cent of all the fresh water discharged into the oceans around the world.

The force of current from this vast volume of water causes the Amazon to flow 125 miles out to sea before it mixes with the Atlantic salt water and early sailors would drink freshwater out of the ocean well before sighting the South American continent. Such is the width and depth of the river that ocean-going ships have navigated as far inland as two-thirds of the way up its entire length.

The Amazon Basin which this massive river system serves to drain - the lion's share of which is in Brazil, but also includes Peru, Colombia, Venezuela, Ecuador, Bolivia, Guyana, Suriname and French Guiana - is famously home to the world's largest rainforest.

The Amazon represents over half the planet's remaining rainforest, and as such is often viewed as the lung of the world.

It is also an ecosystem with unparalleled biodiversity . This is in part because of its tropical nature, and in part because of its history. It was at times an inland sea, and at times a collection of isolated islands of forest separated by savanna, which allowed a divergence in the evolution of species. To date, at least 40,000 plant species have been scientifically classified in the region, together with 3,000 fish, 1,294 bird, 427 mammal, 428 amphibian and 378 reptile species.

And then there are the human beings who live in the forest. The Brazilian Amazon alone is home to some 20 million people, the majority of whom live in cities and towns, although there are still 400 different indigenous groups living in the forest including a few who have had no contact with the outside world.

There was a time when the number of indigenous groups of people was far greater. Many were destroyed by epidemics as a result of the early construction of highways and human settlements, and many more continue to be threatened by the deforestation of large tracts of the Amazon for logging, cattle ranching and soybean production.

Today, while indigenous people continue to fight for their cultural survival and the biodiversity of the forest upon which their lives depend, environmentalists are also concerned about the release of the carbon contained within the vegetation which many believe is accelerating global warming.

"The force of current from the Amazon's vast volume of water flows 125 miles out to sea before it mixes with the Atlantic salt water. Early sailors would drink freshwater out of the ocean well before sighting the South American continent."

PERU

"The Sacred Valley of the Incas was exquisite. High mountains with fertile valleys, but also an incredibly harsh way of life."

Continuing their journey inland along the Amazon into Peru, Joanna and Steve eventually reached Iquitos, a major Amazonian port, where they were greeted by perplexed officials who claimed to have no prior warning of their arrival.

Old hands by now at dealing with bureaucracy, they were soon battling their way through the crowded streets before embarking on another adventure, this time by boat along one of the Amazon's many tributaries, to meet the local Yakuas people. Never one to pass up such a golden opportunity, Joanna was soon hard at work documenting her impressions on film.

Partly because they needed a few days rest after their gruelling flight along the Amazon - and partly because they had considerable problems tracking down some more fuel! - they were also able to spend some time in The Lost Valley of the Incas, east of Cusco. It was a magical few days and the perfect opportunity to recharge their batteries ready for the final stage of their journey.

Flight Information

FLIGHT DISTANCE	1,729NM
FLIGHT TIME	14HRS 58MINS

ENTRY:S04° 06.39′ W70° 00.50′.   EXIT:S12° 46.22′ W68° 51.12′.

146

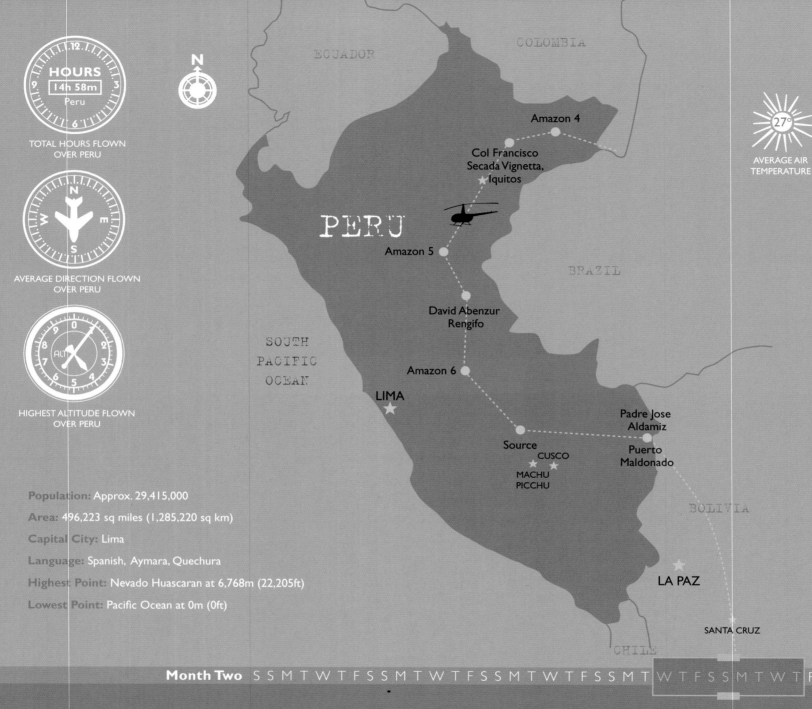

HOURS
14h 58m
Peru

TOTAL HOURS FLOWN
OVER PERU

N

AVERAGE DIRECTION FLOWN
OVER PERU

HIGHEST ALTITUDE FLOWN
OVER PERU

27°

AVERAGE AIR
TEMPERATURE

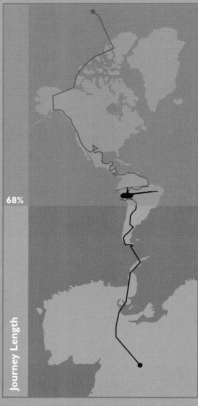

ECUADOR

COLOMBIA

Amazon 4

Col Francisco
Secada Vignetta,
Iquitos

PERU

Amazon 5

BRAZIL

David Abenzur
Rengifo

SOUTH
PACIFIC
OCEAN

Amazon 6

LIMA

Padre Jose
Aldamiz

Source
CUSCO

Puerto
Maldonado

MACHU
PICCHU

BOLIVIA

LA PAZ

SANTA CRUZ

CHILE

68%

Journey Length

Cumulative Distance: 14,365nm
Cumulative Time: 124hrs 21mins

Population: Approx. 29,415,000

Area: 496,223 sq miles (1,285,220 sq km)

Capital City: Lima

Language: Spanish, Aymara, Quechura

Highest Point: Nevado Huascaran at 6,768m (22,205ft)

Lowest Point: Pacific Ocean at 0m (0ft)

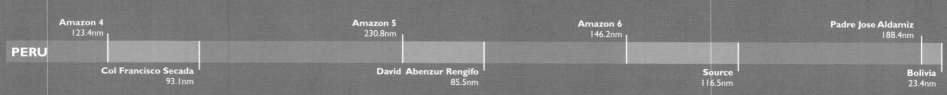

Month Two   S S M T W T F S S M T W T F S S M T W T F S S M T W T F S S M T W T F S S

Amazon 4 123.4nm		Amazon 5 230.8nm		Amazon 6 146.2nm		Padre Jose Aldamiz 188.4nm
PERU	Col Francisco Secada 93.1nm		David Abenzur Rengifo 85.5nm		Source 116.5nm	Bolivia 23.4nm

Diary

In its rubber boom heyday, Iquitos was among the richest cities in the world and is still a major Amazonian port, with a population of some 400,000. It is also one of the most populous cities in the world that is accessible only by boat or plane (or helicopter), but not the common car.

"The city was teeming," says Joanna. "We were met by a crowd of people while still on the tarmac at the airport. None seemed to have the first clue what to do with us. The Aeronautical Information Service apparently had no record of our permit; there were drug enforcement police telling us how dangerous it was to fly; and no Avgas, so we couldn't fly even had we wanted to!"

"It seemed a little unusual, too," adds Steve, "that one of the people who greeted us was a policeman who turned out also to be a tour guide." And an illustration of Joanna's and Steve's trusting state of mind that they jumped aboard a rickshaw with this man, and motored through the humid, crowded streets of Iquitos - a cacophony of bike engines and horns blasting in their ears - to the water's edge, where a boat awaited them.

The policeman took them to an Amazonian village, home to the indigenous Yakuas people. Together they stepped aboard a long and narrow river boat - driver in the stern with a long-shaft propeller in hand - and sped along the winding tributaries of the Amazon. "The sun was setting, mosquitoes biting," says Steve, "and there was a hell of a din of squawks and screeches coming from the forest."

The boat drew up to a bank, close to the Yakuas village. "Rather oddly, self-consciously, the policeman began to whistle," says Joanna. "We went into a small clearing in the forest, reed huts around the edges.

People emerged from all around, with feather headdresses and painted faces. Soon the drums were rolling. They anointed our faces and we danced." Here Joanna and Steve indulged in one of the few purchases of their trip: a tribal necklace of parrot feathers to hang over G-NUDE's GPS and donated a little money for medicine.

About to board the boat once more, Steve realised that he had left his sunglasses in the village and, much to his surprise, returned to see one of the dancers slip on a pair of Nikes behind a hut. So Joanna's suspicion had been grounded: the policeman's self-conscious whistle had been to alert the villagers to prepare for their visitors, to change from Western to tribal dress - one way of mediating between two very different worlds.

Later Joanna was able to speak to a woman from one of the local tribes. She was happy, she said, if her children went to school and worked in Iquitos as long as they learned and passed on through the generations, the language, songs and dance, so central to the tribe's identity. A man from another village explained how he and his family performed to tourists in a mock-up village easily accessible from the river. Meanwhile, they retained their privacy in another community deep in the forest.

Joanna's anthropological curiosity tugged at her to stay a little longer, but her desire to complete a journey started - Steve's too - urged them on. They managed, with effort, to locate some Avgas at a small fishing village upstream, and after exhausting negotiations with the Peruvian flight authorities, were granted permission to continue their journey south along the Ucayali River, a major headwater of the Amazon.

This brought them to Pucallpa and on again, south and east, over mile upon mile of dense rainforest to the sizeable town of Puerto Maldonado, close to the Bolivian border. Before landing here, Joanna

and Steve had made a decision: they needed a break. They perhaps hadn't appreciated the level of exhaustion accrued from their focussed and prolonged flight over the Amazonian rainforest, but certainly Joanna had had her fill of Peruvian bureaucracy.

"Not only do they charge huge landing and communication fees, but they also extort money for every kilometre you fly! Brazil was expensive, but Peru almost finished us off! Hours and hours of waiting for pretty poor service." There was another issue as well, which they couldn't possibly have foreseen. Puerto Maldonado, despite having an airport and a raft of gas-guzzling industries, had not a single drop of Avgas. "We'd hit the end of the road," says Steve, "No Avgas, no flying."

They needed a solution, and typically for our pair of pilots, their search encompassed a good dollop of exploration and fun as well. Machu Picchu is a 'must-see' in Peru. They booked commercial flights to the highland town of Cusco, launch pad to this Lost City of the Incas and also, they hoped, a town of sufficient size to be home to at least one supplier of Avgas.

"It had been a while since we'd been surrounded by so many tourists," says Joanna, "every street jammed with internet cafes and shops selling souvenirs, postcards, white water rafting, pony trekking, all sorts. We were a bit stunned, to be honest. But we spent some time with a wonderful guide, visiting a few small pueblos around Pisac in the Sacred Valley of the Incas. It was exquisite - high, the air fresh, an oasis of fertile valleys - but also an

incredibly harsh way of life. The families are big; the children help on the farms. But few have access to schools and health care."

Back in Cusco, their adventure through the winding, narrow backstreets in search of Avgas proved a delightful affirmation of the resourcefulness, and trustworthiness, of the Peruvian people. "We managed to explain to our taxi driver that we needed to find a gas station that sold 95 octane fuel, a single barrel to transport it in, and a trucking company," explains Joanna.

"Completely unfazed, he drove us through town - children everywhere, stray dogs, the odd llama - and after two or three enquiries, found a yard where they agreed to sell us a barrel for 40 pesos. It was a bit oily but the boys sorted that, swilling some fuel around the inside of the barrel. We then drove to a petrol station and filled it with fuel while it lay in the back of the taxi."

"Next stop: a trucking company," Joanna continues. "Amazingly a guy agreed to drive it all the way to Puerto Maldonado - four days drive, horrendous roads - again for 40 pesos. We were taking the plane! Four days later, back in Puerto Maldonado, and there, parked next to Nudie, was the 50 gallon barrel."

They were on the home straight now. Joanna may have chosen not to tell her father it was only car fuel, not aviation fuel, they were now pouring into G-NUDE's tank; but otherwise he might have allowed himself to relax a little. The Amazonian rainforest was almost behind them.

"After exhausting negotiations with the Peruvian flight authorities, they were granted permission to continue their journey south along the Ucayali River, a major headwater of the Amazon."

LOST CITIES OF THE INCAS

Mention Peru and it's difficult not to mention Machu Picchu in the same breath. The Lost City of the Incas, veiled in dense foliage and hidden from the outside world for three centuries and more, was discovered by the American archaeologist, Hiram Bingham, in 1911. Today, the ruins of its fine stone buildings and terraces, perched on a high precipice at nearly 8,000ft between steep Andean peaks overlooking the Urubamba River, create the appearance of a settlement literally carved from the mountainside.

It is one of the most striking archaeological monuments in the world. And yet the Spanish conquistadors, led by Francisco Pizarro in the 1500s, never set eyes on it. Bingham speculated that a remnant of the Inca nobility took refuge here after their empire was destroyed. Later investigators concluded it was home to a military garrison. But sustaining the eerie without an empire proved impossible, and its occupants melted away into the surrounding forest, which in turn took hold and concealed the once-fortified city for over 300 years.

The story of the city of Cusco, just 50 miles from Machu Picchu, is very different. At its peak, the Inca Empire spanned 2,500 miles across modern-day Ecuador, Peru and northern Chile. Cusco was the empire's capital. It was the richest city in the Americas with temples gleaming in gold until the Inca civilization came into direct conflict with European expansion.

Today a walk through Cusco's streets reveal the layers of history: Spanish colonial buildings erected atop Inca walls line the square, while the city is surrounded by Inca ruins, the most impressive being the fortress of Sacsayhuaman, the site of the 1536 battle in which dozens of Pizarro's men charged uphill to do battle with the defending Inca warriors.

Sacsayhuaman is one of the most outstanding examples of the construction skills of Inca workmen. The walls comprise enormous cut-stone blocks that fit so snugly that the finest of knives can't be passed between them: no mortar was used but still the walls stand stable. The technique was to repeatedly lower one rock onto another, patiently carving away any sections on the lower rock where the dust was compressed.

The Incas were also accomplished agriculturists. A short taxi ride from Cusco (and overlooked by Machu Picchu) is the Sacred Valley of the Incas (the Urubamba Valley) which includes numerous archaeological ruins and villages, such as Chinchero, Ollantaytambo, and Pisac. The valley was undoubtedly a key area of settlement for the Incas. It was the route to the tropical lowlands, an area with access to an array of exotic fruits and plants, as well as acting as a buffer zone, protecting Cusco from the incursions of the Antic, fierce jungle tribes who from time to time raided the highlands.

"Bingham speculated that a remnant of the Inca nobility took refuge here after their empire was destroyed and later investigators concluded it was home to a military garrison."

152

ARGENTINA

"It was an instant love affair with this most European of South American countries. The whole place seemed to be alive with the best of a by-gone era."

Of the many great characters Joanna and Steve encountered on their journey south, few made such a powerful and instant impression as the magnetic personalities they met in Argentina.

It all began on their first night on Argentine soil when a potentially serious misunderstanding with the airport authorities was resolved by the arrival of one of the world's most elegant and charming customs official. It was an encounter that was to set the tone for the rest of their stay.

One of the most stylish cultures in South America, Argentina is home to both tango and, at the other end of the spectrum, the nomadic and flamboyant gauchos, renowned the world over for their horsemanship. Both struck a deep chord with Joanna and Steve leading them to spend time in one of the oldest estancias in the country where they were privileged enough to ride out both with the owner and the gauchos.

After a short stay in the capital, Buenos Aires - and Steve's first real connection with the passion that is tango - they were soon flying south once more towards Patagonia and the remote, wind-battered coast of Tierra del Fuego. The end was at last in sight.

Flight Information

FLIGHT DISTANCE	2,751NM
FLIGHT TIME	25HRS 3MIN

ENTRY: S22° 00.09′ W63° 41.24′.   EXIT: S54° 36.56′ W68° 37.80′.

TOTAL HOURS FLOWN
OVER ARGENTINA

AVERAGE DIRECTION FLOWN
OVER ARGENTINA

HIGHEST ALTITUDE FLOWN
OVER ARGENTINA

N

Population: Approx. 40,482,000

Area: 1,073,514 sq miles (2,766,890 sq km)

Capital City: Buenos Aires

Language: Spanish, Guaraní

Highest Point: Cerro Aconcagua (highest mountain

in the Americas) at 6,960m (22,835ft)

Lowest Point: Salinas Chicas at -40m (-164ft)

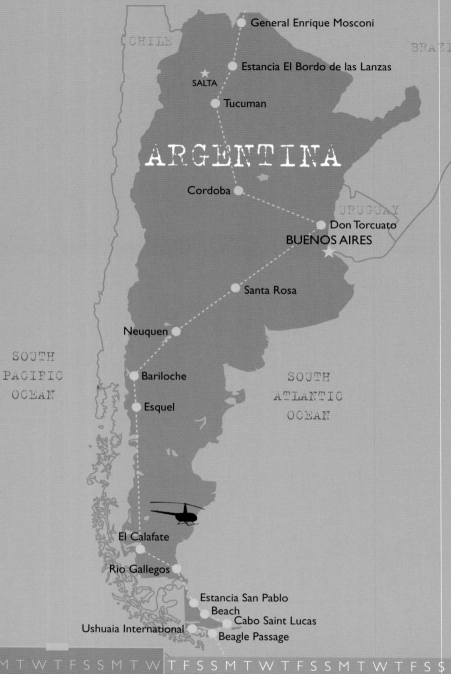

General Enrique Mosconi

Estancia El Bordo de las Lanzas

SALTA

Tucuman

ARGENTINA

Cordoba

Don Torcuato

BUENOS AIRES

Santa Rosa

Neuquen

SOUTH
PACIFIC
OCEAN

Bariloche

Esquel

SOUTH
ATLANTIC
OCEAN

El Calafate

Rio Gallegos

Estancia San Pablo
Beach

Cabo Saint Lucas

Ushuaia International

Beagle Passage

CHILE

BRAZIL

URUGUAY

85%

Journey Length

Cumulative Distance: 17,117nm
Cumulative Time: 149hrs 24mins

26°

AVERAGE AIR
TEMPERATURE

Month Three F S S M T W T F S S M T W T F S S M T W T F S S M T W T F S S M T W T F S S

General
Enrique
Mosconi
38.3nm

ARGENTINA

Benjamin
Matienzo
120.7nm

Don Torcuato
340.8nm

Presidente Peron
232nm

Esquel
105.4nm

Norberto Fernandez
130.7nm

Estancia
San
Pablo
38.5nm

Cabo
Saint Ushuaia
Lucas Intl
25.8nm 63.7nm

Estancia El Bordo
de las Lanzas
19.8nm

Cordoba
272.2nm

Santa Rosa
304nm

S C De Bariloche
190.9nm

El Calafate
444nm

Rio Gallegos
242nm

Beach
46nm

Beagle
Passage
50.9nm

Chile
18.2nm

Flying south and east from Puerto Maldonado, across the Bolivian border to Santa Cruz, the forest thinned. "At last!" cries Steve. "Two weeks of stressful flying over dense canopy and river, and there before us was a vast open plain with gentle hills, and streams, and cattle - landing spots everywhere!"

Just one night in the capital Santa Cruz and Joanna and Steve were moving on again, to Argentina. The day was Sunday; customs officials, not surprisingly, were a little relaxed or indeed absent altogether. It was testament to Joanna's and Steve's persuasive powers that they were able to lift G-NUDE off the ground at all, but inevitably their departure was delayed and as darkness closed in like a blanket thrown across the sky, they were still heading towards Salta,

the capital of Argentina's north-western province, in the foothills of the Andes.

"We were surrounded by huge granite cliffs as black as the sky itself," says Steve. "We had to work as one in the cockpit, seamlessly, faultlessly. Any mistake could have been disastrous." "And we had no radio contact," adds Joanna. "We were 30 miles out of Salta, then 20 miles, but still no radio contact. We frantically tried different

frequencies. Still no response. In the end we just had to make blind calls giving our position and intentions, expected time of arrival, and so on, and just hope someone might pick it up."

In the end they landed, after a perfect night approach on the part of Steve, on a proper-sized international runway, and parked outside the terminal. The airport officials were not best pleased. Why were they late?

Why didn't they radio? Misunderstandings that were further compounded when Joanna and Steve learned the customs and immigration officials had gone home for the night. They were obliged to wait two hours, standing on the runway, while the customs and immigration officials returned.

It was close to 11 o'clock at night and they were exhausted. "But all was forgiven," says Steve, "when the customs lady finally arrived

and greeted us with a kiss on each cheek. So elegant, so beautifully dressed, so vital." It was the beginning of a love affair with this most European of South American countries, "so cultured and old-world", adds Steve, "the whole society seems to retain the best of a by-gone era."

Salta la Linda, 'Salta the Beautiful', is, as its name suggests, a wonderfully atmospheric colonial city with cathedral, museums and, Joanna adds, "shops selling the most fantastic silver and leather. Outrageously cheap!"

Cheap because their visit, in September 2002, was at the tail end of a year that had seen the most devastating economic crisis in Argentina's history. A bitter four-year recession with foreign debt piling up to $150 billion - almost one third of that owed collectively by all developing countries - had led to four presidents resigning in as many months and the peso, once artificially tied to the U.S. dollar at a parity of one to one, free-falling in value.

"We had a fabulous dinner that evening: champagne, steak, red wine. It cost 100 pesos for the pair of us; about U.S.$30. We felt almost guilty about the exchange," says Joanna.

They wanted to see more of Argentina, off the tourist trail as far as it were possible, and the following morning made enquiries at a travel agent. This led very quickly to a cup of coffee with a local man, Augustine Arias, and within half-an-hour they were jumping in G-NUDE and flying, Augustine in the back, to Estancia el Bordo de las Lanzas, one of the oldest farms in the north of Argentina.

Augustine introduced them to his father, Juan Jose Arias. He was the eighth generation of the Arias family to have owned the estancia, now operational as a cattle ranch and also growing sugar cane and tobacco. Joanna and Steve rode

with him that evening through fields of burnt cane, and into vast open grassland, cows scattered with their calves.

"It's hard to get your head around the scale of things from a European viewpoint," says Steve, a man from farming stock himself. "How do they manage if a calf gets stuck during birth, for example? The answer is they don't. They let it die, or else shoot it. They don't want to perpetuate any weakness and as a consequence rarely have any birthing problems. It's tough; these guys are very much in touch with nature," he says, admiration in his voice.

Come evening and they dressed for dinner, drank gins and tonic on the veranda and moved into the estancia's formal dining room; the furniture dark and solid, the silver plentiful, family portraits looking down from the walls as they ate. The place was steeped in colonial history. Sons, daughters, grandmothers, dipped in and out of the conversation all the while. "Just charming," says an enchanted Steve, "a world gone by, one with different worries to our own, worries about the land."

The next morning they tacked up and rode out with Jose, one of the gauchos on the estancia. They rode for two hours under the midday sun, and then into the forest, stopping at a clearing by a stream. Jose positioned their saddles on the ground as seats and Joanna and Steve unbuckled their oversized chaps - tough, thick slabs of hide worn around their legs as protection from the scrub and thorns - and threw them on the earth as a picnic rug.

They gathered firewood, lit a fire; and Jose, lifting large steaks from his saddlebag, skewered them on sharpened sticks and doused them with salt, and balanced them on stones a foot or so above the embers of the fire. "Lunch in 10 minutes?" quizzed a hungry Steve, familiar with the idea of a steak cooking in just a few minutes.

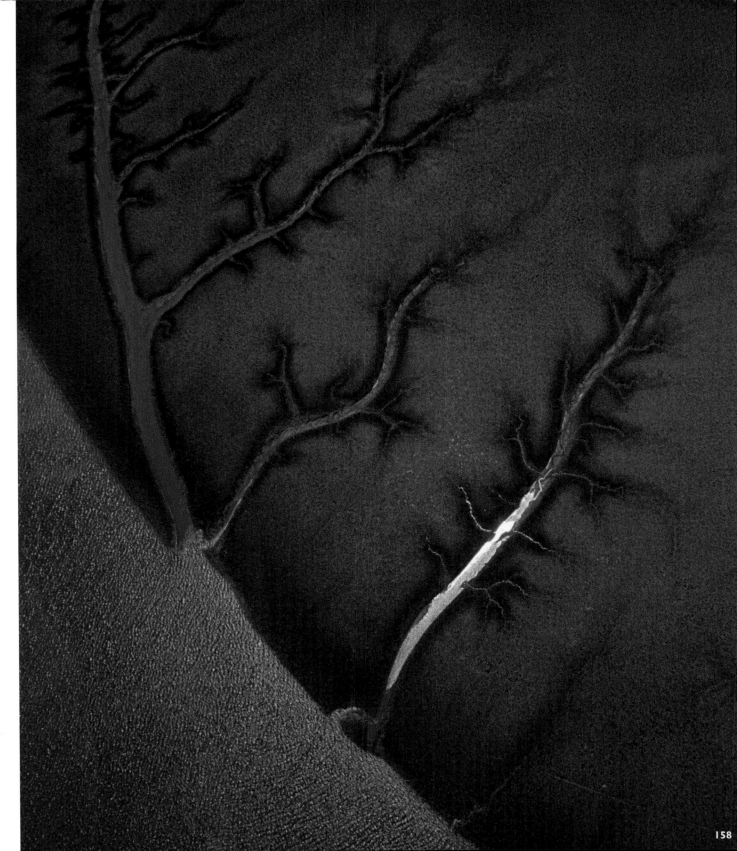

"More like an hour and 10 minutes," Jose answered, and still the steaks were pink in the middle. "Perfect," says Steve, "better than I've tasted anywhere in the world." They ate and drank - red wine magically produced from the saddlebag - and lay back and slept in the afternoon sun, like a pride of well-fed lion.

It was a tough call to leave Estancia el Bordo de las Lanzas and its old traditions; it was a place they knew would lure them back again in time. But for now they had a long journey ahead of them: some 1,500 miles south and east over the seemingly endless grassy plains of the pampas and rich, fertile fields of sugarcane, rice, tobacco and fruit, to Buenos Aires, the vibrant, colourful capital city of Argentina, famous for its tango and free-wheeling, grown-up sophistication.

G-NUDE was in need of a service - an excuse to hang out for a few days. Not to forget that these were politically troubled times. Many of the shops were boarded up. Professional, besuited individuals were driven to scouring the bins for a newspaper, or anything they might be able to recycle for a few pesos. And yet seemingly nothing could destroy their pride, expressed in the way they dressed, the way they carried themselves, and their hospitality.

"We spoke to many Argentineans who felt marooned from the rest of the world because of the astronomically inflated price of airline tickets," says Steve. "They were really happy to see us. We could have been part of their family, the way they treated us. Nothing was too much trouble for them."

They wandered the streets of San Telmo Faria with its flea market and cafés and musicians, jazz and tango permeating the streets, and visited La Boca, a suburb originally settled by immigrants from Italy and Spain, and the place where tango was born among the colourful and picturesque bordellos. Come evening, reluctantly in the case of Steve, they dropped into a club well-trodden on the tourist trail, to watch tango in action. "Once again I was inspired to my core; I had tears rolling down my face," he confesses, "so soul-lifting and passionate."

From Argentina's capital, Joanna and Steve took a zigzag south and back west to San Carlos de Bariloche in the Andean foothills - a journey that took them two days. Bariloche, affectionately called 'Little Switzerland' with its chocolate shops and dulce de leche served in every café, is Argentina's major ski resort. Joanna and Steve enjoyed a couple of days whistling down snow-capped mountains of extraordinary beauty, "with views over countless lakes and islands in shades of emerald green and purple," says Joanna.

They toyed with the idea, from here, of hopping west over the border into Chile to refuel before continuing their journey south, but the requisite red tape surrounding customs and immigration rather put them off. Instead they opted to stay in Argentina and fly directly south, 100 miles or so, to Esquel, and there fill G-NUDE's tank to the brim for a flight of 440 miles due south again to El Calafate.

They were now in Patagonia and the winds, they had been told, would be horrendous. "440 miles was at the edge of NUDE's range," explains Steve, "and she was flying heavy with fuel. But actually, on this occasion, the wind worked to our advantage. It was blowing across a flat valley from the north east and sweeping up as it hit the hills. We were being lifted and blown south by nature, down the eastern foothills of the Andes, in winds of up to 60mph, almost gliding along the ridge."

"And the scenery just got better and better," adds Joanna, "over snow-capped mountains and through completely untouched valleys, just the odd sheep estancia breaking the natural horizon. We took time to stop by a lake, breathtakingly beautiful, surrounded by smooth clean rock, just to take in the view."

"The outside air temperature was below zero - in sharp contrast to their flight over equatorial rainforest just a couple of weeks before."

The outside air temperature was below zero - in sharp contrast to their flight over equatorial rainforest, just a couple of weeks before. Their flight, mile after mile, just a couple of hundred feet above the Earth's surface, had enabled them to see, smell, and feel the climate as it changed from an extreme northerly latitude, through temperate and tropical zones, and back to a temperate climate again as they approached the extreme south. Theirs was the understanding of the scale and curvature of the Earth.

Four hours in the air, and another two bumping along the rough roads of southern Patagonia, and they checked in at Hosteria Los Notros, one of the most exclusive hotels in Argentina, not famed for its décor, particularly, or its sophistication, but for its position. Lie in the bath, or in the bed of your private room, and the view through the window is of the infinitely mysterious Perito Moreno glacier, flowing into the milky turquoise waters of Lago Argentino. As if a mirror had been held up on the equator, Joanna and Steve were back where their travels had begun, gazing out at a glacier.

Their journey as a honeymoon couple was drawing to a close. From El Calafate they flew south and east, stopping at Rio Gallegos only to refuel, before flying across the Magellan Straits to Río Grande, Tierra del Fuego. A posse of pilots at the local aero club - as always, generous to the cause - dug out a dusty chart marked with estancias that welcomed flying visitors.

For three days Joanna and Steve rested at Cabo San Pablo, an estancia run by Juan Carlos Apolinaire and his Welsh wife Rachel

Apolinaire, on the wind-battered easterly coast of Tierra del Fuego. It was easily spotted. From the air they could see an oversized number '50' painted in white on the rust red tin roof of the sheep shearing station. From here there is nothing but open sea to the Falkland Islands. During the Falklands War, apparently, the roof of each estancia's shearing shed was marked with such a number, as a navigational aid for the fighter pilots on their return from action.

It was, and truly felt, as if it were at the end of the world. Cabo San Pablo was the most southerly estancia, still inhabited, along this desolate stretch of coast; the nearest shop was three hours drive away. Once, its 21,000 acres had yielded a decent return; but with the demise of the wool trade and demand for Argentinean lamb, it was as hard now to eke a living from the land as it was for the young saplings to grow straight and tall in the cold, unrelenting wind howling off the South Atlantic.

At every turn there were shadows of harsh lives carved in a harsh environment, with nature winning in the end: estancias abandoned; a seal pelt factory, its wooden sheds desiccated and caved in like a heap of matchsticks, machinery rusted and broken. But for Joanna and Steve there was a beauty in the landscape, too - in the peat bogs and pebbled beaches, and brave, battered flag trees, gnarled and sculptured by the wind. And above all, there was freedom. At last, in this frontier land, they were out of radio transmission range of any of the aviation authorities and, finally, they felt they could fly where they liked, when they liked, hopping here and there, unpestered.

"We were surrounded by huge granite cliffs and had to work as one in the cockpit, seamlessly, faultlessly. Any mistake could have been disastrous."

LAND OF THE GAUCHOS

Wherever there are cattle, and cattle ranches, there are people on horseback to tend to them. In the U.S. there are cowboys; in Chile, huasos; in Colombia and Venezuela, llaneros; and, on the wide open pampas of Argentina, Uruguay and southern Brazil, there are gauchos.

The word gaucho comes from the Quechua word 'huachu', meaning 'orphan' or 'vagabond', which speaks volumes for their early reputation. Gauchos were nomadic. From the 1600s, they shunned the convention of settlement and town, choosing instead the freedom of the open skies and sun-baked pampas, living off the grassland and gathering together in vaquerias to hunt. Some of the gauchos might have had a simple home, with common-law wife, even offspring, but little time was spent there.

Their flamboyant dress (much the same today as of old) reflected their life on horseback: a poncho, which doubled up as a saddle blanket and sleeping gear, loose fitting trousers called bombachas, belted with a tirador or chiripa, and knee-high boots fashioned by wrapping the hide of a freshly killed calf around the legs and feet until it dried, moulded to the shape of the owner. A typical gaucho owned nothing of value except his beloved horse, a facon (large knife), a rebenque (whip) and a boleodoras, comprising a triplet of stones bound in leather straps used to trip cattle.

Interestingly, in the early days it wasn't the meat from cattle that was of value - just the leather, which could be traded across oceans without deteriorating. The meat had to be eaten quickly (if it wasn't

to go off in the heat) and this the gauchos perfected, grilling it over an open fire - a cooking method which is something of a national pastime today, but which then was regarded as distasteful, uncouth, only adding to their rough, heavy-mannered image. The gambling and several-times-a-day ritual of drinking yerbe mate, a mildly narcotic concoction drunk from a gourd, perhaps didn't help either.

However, in the early 1800s the image of the gaucho underwent a transformation. During the War of Independence against Spain, when commanders looked for able-bodied men, the gauchos - fine, hardy horsemen with an intricate knowledge of the land - were called into service where their fighting skills and loyalty quickly commanded the respect of the military.

As settlements grew in the interior of the newly-independent Argentina, the gauchos at first resisted the encroachment that threatened their solitary ways. But with time, employment on the great ranches was irresistible; they settled, rounded cattle, fixed fences, branded animals. And today they can still be seen - about 150,000 in number - galloping alongside the road, hair and poncho flying, performing valuable seasonal work on the estancias and exhibiting their considerable horse handling skills at the country bordilleros.

As they have integrated, so the legend of the gaucho has grown. A romantic image of the past, the gaucho represents freedom from colonial control. In Argentina, June 16th is a holiday, celebrating the guachos contribution to the War of Independence. Also a hero of the present, the gaucho represents freedom from social constraints.

"The flamboyant dress reflected their life on horseback: a poncho, loose fitting trousers called bombachas, and knee-high boots fashioned by wrapping the hide of a freshly killed calf around the legs and feet until it dried, moulded to the shape of the owner."

CHILE

"The end of the world as we know it. We were back in the land of snow and ice once more."

With the end of their odyssey finally in sight, in many ways Steve and Joanna found themselves back where they had started. Snow-capped mountains and frozen landscapes surrounded them as they made their way to the tip of South America with sub-zero temperatures and drifting snow once again the norm.

After leaving Ushuaia in Argentina, the world's most southerly city, they made their way north again over the bleak beauty of the frozen fjords, mountains and lakes of Tierra del Fuego, a vast archipelago made up of one large island, Isla Grande (split 60/40 between Chile and Argentina), and a group of off-lying smaller ones.

Their final goal now was Punta Arenas, another city teetering

on the edge the world, where they had arranged to park G-NUDE after their three-month, 15,000-mile odyssey from Alaska to the southern tip of Chile.

But while Joanna's extraordinary journey was at last over, for Steve there remained one further challenge: a first flight in a single-engine helicopter over the infamous Drake Passage to Antarctica.

Flight Information

FLIGHT DISTANCE	64NM
FLIGHT TIME	33MINS

ENTRY:S54° 36.56′ W68° 37.80′.   EXIT:S55° 10.25′ W66° 20.57′.

166

HOURS
0h 33m
Chile

TOTAL HOURS FLOWN
OVER CHILE

AVERAGE DIRECTION FLOWN
OVER CHILE

HIGHEST ALTITUDE FLOWN
OVER CHILE

N

CHILE

ARGENTINA

BRAZIL

URUGUAY

SANTIAGO ★

SOUTH
PACIFIC
OCEAN

SOUTH
ATLANTIC
OCEAN

Population: Approx. 16,454,000

Area: 291,933 sq miles (756,102 sq km)

Capital City: Santiago

Language: Spanish

Highest Point: Cerro Aconcagua at 6,962m (22,841ft)

Lowest Point: Pacific Ocean at 0m (0ft)

PUNTA ARENAS ★

⬤ Ushuaia Intl

88%

Journey Length

Cumulative Distance: 17,180nm
Cumulative Time: 149hrs 57mins

14°

AVERAGE AIR
TEMPERATURE

Month Three F S S M T W T F S S M T W T F S S M T W T F S S M T W T F S S M T W T F S S

WP 1
119.5nm

WP 2
63.7nm

CHILE

Ushuaia Intl Malvine Is
137.6nm

ANTARCTICA
9.5nm

S o close to their final destination now. Still in Argentina, they turned west along the Beagle Channel to the bayside city of Ushuaia, the most southerly city in the world. It might, logically, have been where their journey concluded, except that they had made prior arrangements to park **G-NUDE** in a hangar

in **Punta Arenas, a journey of some 142 nautical miles north and west over fjords, mountains, lakes and the Chilean border.**

The weather wasn't on their side for the last leg of their journey. They found themselves flying into a strong head wind, one that increased fuel consumption and strained the pilots' nerves as they twisted and

turned along a small meandering river into a rapidly narrowing valley, a ceiling of menacing cloud overhead. But finally there was a glimmer of light at the other end. The valley broadened and there ahead was an open lake with mountains all around.

Still, the sky was patchy with cloud but fortunately the direction they

were due to fly was clear. They scraped through a mountain pass and, at last, along the coastline of the Magellan Straits to Punta Arenas. On the afternoon of October 2nd, 2002, after three months in the sky, they finally landed safely, their epic 15,000 mile journey from Alaska down the length of the Americas to the southern tip of Chile at an end.

"We were utterly exhausted," says Joanna, "we slept for days." "And yet it was the most tremendous sense of achievement," Steve concludes. "Our planet was once something that we'd pored over in an atlas, and was now something we had tasted, felt, touched. There was a big sense of privilege. And we'd survived, too. That was the greatest privilege of all!"

But Joanna and Steve both knew the journey wasn't over yet. G-NUDE would rest a while in a hangar in Punta Arenas, but it wouldn't be long before Steve was back with his friend and instructor Q to attempt a single-engine helicopter flight that nobody had accomplished before. The final leg of their epic journey: a flight across the Drake Passage to Antarctica and the South Pole.

THE DRAKE PASSAGE

To the English-speaking world, the stretch of water between South America and Antarctica is the Drake Passage, named after Sir Francis Drake, who in 1578, in the course of circumnavigating the world, passed through the Strait of Magellan into the Pacific Ocean. Before he could continue his voyage north, he was hit by a storm and was blown well to the south of Tierra del Fuego, leading him to suppose that far from being another continent, as previously believed, Tierra del Fuego was in fact an island with open sea to the south.

For the Spanish and Latin Americans, the same stretch of water is called Mar de Hoces, after the Spanish navigator Francisco de Hoces, who, half a century earlier, was blown south by a gale in front of the Atlantic end of the Strait of Magellan and reached 56°S where he and his crew "thought to see Land's End".

Whatever you call it, there is no argument: this body of water is one of the most treacherous stretches of ocean in the world. Nor that the brave navigator who first sailed through it was a Dutchman, Willem Schouten, in his ship Eendracht in 1616. It was after his home town, Hoorn, that the most southerly point of South America was called Kaap Hoorn, or Cape Horn.

The Drake Passage is some 480 miles wide at its narrowest point between Cape Horn and Greenwich Island off the coast of Antarctica - but it wasn't always so. Until around 40 million years ago the passage was closed, the Atlantic and Pacific Oceans separate, and the Antarctic warm. When the passage opened, the two great oceans joined and the Antarctic Circumpolar Current was set into motion, cooling the continent significantly.

Today the current, unimpeded by any block of land, flows round and round Antarctica, west to east, constricted only where it squeezes through the relatively narrow jaws of the Drake Passage - just one factor that contributes to the Drake's fearsome reputation as one of the most hazardous shipping routes in the world.

Other factors include hurricane-force winds, monstrous waves, and icebergs. Just as the current flows unimpeded around Antarctica, so too do the prevailing winds, with cyclonic lows literally chasing each other around the world. Sailors commonly share stories of the 'roaring forties': violent winds encountered at latitudes below 40°S; but Cape Horn requires sailors to push further south still, to latitudes of 56°S, into the 'furious fifties'.

Funnelled through the Drake with the Andes Mountains to the north and Antarctic Peninsula to the south, the wind is exacerbated still further. Add to this, waves running from two and sometimes three different directions as a result of the Pacific and Atlantic Oceans converging and the result is a stretch of water so chaotic and dangerous that today, as yesterday, even the saltiest of dogs approach with trepidation.

"Whatever you call it, there is no argument that this body of water is one of the most treacherous stretches of ocean in the world."

ANTARCTICA

No other place on Earth comes close to the challenges faced by those who are brave, or foolhardy, enough to take on Antarctica. But only the Drake Passage and the Antarctic mainland now separated Steve from his dream of flying a helicopter from Pole to Pole. Having come so far, he was not to be denied. Or so he hoped.

SOUTH POLE

"The North Pole was a frozen ocean surrounded by land. Now we were facing a frozen continent surrounded by a sea with a truly formidable reputation."

Never one to refuse a challenge, Steve was determined to return to Chile and finish the journey he had started with Q at the North Pole and had continued with Joanna from Alaska to the very tip of South America. And after finally convincing the U.K. and Chilean authorities that a flight to Antarctica across the Drake Passage in a single-engine helicopter, one of the most treacherous stretches of water in the world, was indeed possible, return he did.

With Q, the ultimate helicopter wizard, alongside him, the pair calmly made meticulous preparations. Logistics were not easy. The Drake Passage is 480 miles wide at its narrowest point and if they were to succeed, and for Steve to be the first person to fly a helicopter from Pole to Pole, there was no room for even the slightest margin of error. On a perfect summer's evening, with all the weather reports in their favour, they set out from Cape Horn and soon had Antarctica tantalisingly in view. To this day, the two pilots are not sure exactly what caused the engine to malfunction. But malfunction it did and within a few short seconds they were hurtling towards the Southern Ocean. What happened next - and Steve's subsequent refusal to admit defeat - has passed into the annals of Antarctic history.

Flight Information

FLIGHT DISTANCE	2,277NM
FLIGHT TIME	19HRS 42MINS

ENTRY: S55° 10.25' W66° 20.57'.   SOUTH POLE: S90° 00.00' E-W00° 00.00'.

TOTAL HOURS FLOWN
OVER ANTARCTICA

AVERAGE DIRECTION FLOWN
OVER ANTARCTICA

HIGHEST ALTITUDE FLOWN
OVER ANTARCTICA

ANTARCTICA

Jabany Base

Vernadsky

Camp 1

Camp 2

SOUTHERN
OCEAN

Camp 3

Patriot Hills

Thiel Mountains

SOUTH POLE

Population: No permanent population

Area: 5,000,000 sq miles (14,000,000 sq km)

Highest Point: Mt. Vincent at 5,140m (16,864ft)

Lowest Point: Southern Ocean at 0m (0ft)

Journey Length

100%

Cumulative Distance: 19,457nm
Cumulative Time: 169hrs 39mins

30°

AVERAGE AIR
TEMPERATURE

Month Three F S S M T W T F S S M T W T F S S M T W T F S S M T W T F S S M T W T F S S

ANTARCTICA

Jabany Base
483.5nm

Camp 1
99.8nm

Camp 3
337.8nm

Thiel Mountains
308.8nm

Venandsky
228.5nm

Camp 2
332.2nm

Patriot Hills
190nm

South Pole
286.6 nm

If the U.K. helicopter fraternity had concerns about Steve and Q flying the aviation equivalent of a small family hatchback across the frozen Arctic Ocean to the North Pole, they were now doubly concerned about their quest to fly the same machine across the Drake Passage, the notoriously treacherous stretch of water separating South America from Antarctica.

"Most people would want to cross water in a twin-engine," says the Editor-in-Chief of Helicopter Life, Georgina Hunter-Jones. "Many wouldn't cross the English Channel because it's too scary." At its narrowest point, the Drake Passage is some 480 miles across compared to the English Channel's 20 miles, and is exposed to the most ferocious weather systems in the world. Vast 30ft high waves roll one after another to the horizon with winds gusting upwards of 125mph.

It has been the graveyard of countless ships and Steve's proposal to fly a single piston-engine helicopter across the Drake Passage was a feat that had never been attempted before - one that was received with apprehension by both the U.K. helicopter fraternity and the Chilean Aviation Authority. The latter expressed extreme caution and at first applied the brakes, denying the pair clearance for the flight, until eventually after lengthy persuasion, they capitulated.

Steve, accompanied by Q, was at last free to pursue the final leg of his quest to be the first person to fly a helicopter from the North to the South Pole. But there was no doubt in his mind - or anybody else's - that crossing the Drake Passage would be the biggest challenge that he and Q had faced to date, and that it would carry by far the greatest risk.

In mid-January, 2003, the pair calmly set about preparing for the trip. From Punta Arenas, they flew the little R44 G-NUDE south and east to Cape Horn, the very southern tip of South America and the launch pad for a crossing of the open sea. Here they dropped a barrel of fuel and flew north to Port Williams to top up G-NUDE's fuel tank, before flying back to Cape Horn and topping

176

"I didn't for one moment believe it was possible to survive ditching in the Southern Ocean. I was convinced I was facing death but I felt calm," says Q, remarkably sanguine.

up the tank again for the last time on South American soil. Then they waited. They needed four-and-a-half hours of clear skies, sufficient time to cross the Drake Passage and land safely at the Chilean Marsh base on King George Island, the largest of the South Shetland Islands just off the Antarctic Peninsula.

At 7 p.m. on the evening of 26th January 2003, the weather looked good and at such extreme southerly latitudes in midsummer, there were no concerns about fading light. "It was a gorgeous evening," says Steve. "We took off and had great tail winds, and a ground speed of about 130 knots. We had a satellite phone on board and made regular half-hour calls to the Chilean Aviation Authority, recording our position. And at one point I called Joanna - I just couldn't resist it."

"He called half way across the Drake Passage, just to say what a beautiful evening it was!" cries an incredulous Joanna. "I told him pretty sharply to wait until they reached the other side and proceeded to walk around the house with a phone in each hand, until eventually I went to bed."

Back in the cockpit of the little helicopter, everything was proceeding as well as the pilots could have hoped. They were eating up the miles over the icy water; altitude 700ft, tail winds a comfortable 30 knots. "At about 11 p.m.," says Steve, "I could just see the sun setting on the hills of the Antarctic Peninsula in the distance. Antarctica was within our grasp."

And then, in a moment, everything changed. "Suddenly there was a rattle in the engine," says Steve. "We looked at each other and said, What's that?" "I don't know, but we're losing power," answered Q. Steve grabbed the GPS. "We're 36 miles north of Smith Island," he shouted above the noise. "I don't think I'm going to be able to hold it that long," Q replied.

The rattle grew louder and louder and then the oil gauge did a slow sweep from high to zero pressure. Then BOOM! There was an audible bang. And then silence. Just the whistle of the air through the rotors.

Time slowed down.

"We were at about 700ft," says Steve, "but both Q and I knew very well that in 15 or 16 seconds we were going to be in the ocean." A catastrophe. Ditching a helicopter in water is a pilot's greatest fear. Put simply, helicopters just don't float. Both Steve and Q knew that the accepted emergency procedure was to stay belted into the helicopter until it sank below the surface of the water, then unclip and swim out. And yet Q had chatted to a number of pilots who had done just that and only managed to successfully evacuate their helicopters by virtue of their settling on the ground, whether that be the bottom of a lake, or a river, or a shallow sea. This part of the Southern Ocean was 12,000ft deep. Steve and Q wouldn't stand a chance.

Because of this, Q had conceived and drilled Steve with a very different evacuation procedure should this most unlikely of events occur while flying across the Drake Passage. It was completely unorthodox and against all accepted wisdom. It was also untested but would, Q hoped, offer them a chance of survival.

"The co-pilot gets out of the helicopter and stands on the skid," explains Q, "with all the equipment required, including a life dinghy. There's a sweet spot in time when the co-pilot can step off the skid and into the water, but he must not jump until the pilot says 'now', and it will feel late, very late," he stresses. "And it's imperative he stays with the dinghy, whatever it takes. Then it's down to the pilot to land the helicopter at zero water speed - gently lay the helicopter into the water - and bale out before it sinks like a stone."

Never did either of them believe they'd have to put this extreme manoeuvre into practice.

The two men looked at each other. They didn't speak. But just registered the extreme urgency of their situation, and set about what they had to do. Q turned G-NUDE into the wind in preparation to land, while unclipping his safety belt and pushing the EPIRB (Emergency Positioning Indicating Radio Beacon) into his survival suit. Steve unclipped and climbed out onto the skid. He reached for the liferaft on the back seat of the cockpit with one hand, grabbed a waterproof bag with satellite phone in the other, and turned to face out to sea.

"Not yet," shouted Q.

They were flying at some 80 knots, about 200ft above the water.

"Not yet!"

Q began to flare the helicopter, speeding up the rotor head as the machine slowed down. He'd done this countless times. It's what he did, teaching others. The curve was infinitesimally smooth; but for Steve, standing on the skid, the horizon tipped. He lost his footing, grabbed the side of the door to steady himself - and dropped the liferaft.

"Not yet!" screamed Q.

But he couldn't know what Steve registered to his horror in an instant. The liferaft had fallen between the skid and the main body of the helicopter and was clipped to him - to his survival suit - by a webbing strap. It pulled at him, tugged at him, flailing about under and behind the belly of the helicopter. There was no chance to unclip. The flailing weight of the liferaft pulled on the fastener and locked it tight. Yet do nothing and Steve faced certain death. Tangled with the helicopter, he was destined to sink with the machine to the ocean floor.

Steve had one option. He jumped. "Being frightened did not occur to me," he says. "There was no time. I just knew it was what I had to do to stay alive." His hope was that the force of his falling body would snap the webbing strap. The water hit. He punctured through the surface, hard, like concrete, and sank deep into the Southern Ocean, the shock of the cold clamping his lungs. "In my mind he was dead," says Q. "Best estimate is that he jumped at 80ft, at a water speed upwards of 70 knots." Whatever, it was too high, too fast, too soon. In Q's words "completely unsurvivable".

So his friend Steve was gone; but so, too, the dinghy - Q's last hope of hanging on to life. He turned the helicopter back towards Steve and the life dinghy. Hands still on the controls, he shifted his weight to the edge of the seat, wedging his body and shoulders in the open door. "I didn't for one moment believe it was possible to survive ditching in the Southern Ocean. I was convinced I was facing death; but I felt calm," he says, remarkably sanguine, "I was also curious. I'd never landed in water before."

Few pilots could have done what Q did in that moment. He brought down the helicopter with perfection, touching the skids of the helicopter onto the surface of the ocean at precisely zero water speed.

"It worked better than I could have imagined," he says, "it was so artistic, and lovely, and quiet. The water anchored the helicopter, cradled it in its form. I sat on the edge of the seat, in my own private bubble, with water filling the cockpit. No wind. Stuff floating. It lasted eight to ten seconds - a long time. Until eventually the rotors ran out of energy and the helicopter started sinking like a stone, like pressing the down button on an elevator. I was wedged in the doorway but the water just peeled the helicopter off me and I was outside it, completely immersed in water - all greys and blues. It was beautiful. I remember thinking that aesthetically it was the right colour for death.

For a moment I hadn't a clue which way was up. Then I followed a bubble to the surface, and felt the helicopter sink past my body."

Q broke the surface, gasping for air. Just a few feet from his body was a wall of fire - fuel burning on the surface. He turned his head and there, some distance away, was Steve. Alive! Steve's gamble had worked; but the liferaft, now separated from him, had automatically inflated and was in danger of being blown away. "I knew without it we'd be dead," says Steve. "It was all so clear in my head. First the liferaft. Then Q."

At his own admission Q isn't a strong swimmer, but the adrenalin kicked in and he clawed his way towards Steve who was now swimming towards him, dragging the dinghy behind him on a rope. "I couldn't understand it," exclaims Steve, "Q kept waving and gesticulating frantically to me. Eventually I turned my head, and then I saw it; a flaming sleeping bag was being blown in the direction of the dinghy!"

Steve let go of the dinghy - "quite an unnatural moment," he confesses - and watched the sleeping bag being blown just inches from the dinghy before he swam to retrieve his lost prize again. Eventually he was able to pull himself, then Q, into the raft. "It was full of water and didn't have a roof but at least we were floating," says an ever-optimistic Steve.

Nonetheless, the stark reality of their situation was inescapable: the success or failure of their expedition - now measurable in stark terms of survival - was dependent not only on their own actions, but that of others. "We had to let someone know we were alive," says Steve. Steve set about making some calls on the satellite phone. He called the Chilean Aviation Authorities, but failed to get through; then Q's father, a helicopter pilot himself, to be greeted by an answerphone. At this point a wave came over and drenched the phone. Alarmingly the lights on the phone went out,

but then flitted back on again. "I remember thinking I've only got a couple of minutes left on this thing," says Steve, "the next call has got to work...so I called Joanna."

It was 3 a.m. in London. Joanna was sound asleep. "The phone rang and it was Steve," she recalls. "Do you have a pen? Two pilots down, 35 miles north of Smith Island, urgent help needed. Both pilots are well," gasped Steve, desperate to give their position before the phone gave out. "What shall I do?" said Joanna. "I don't know, dial 999, whatever..." Steve replied. And the phone went dead.

In that moment another wave swamped the little liferaft and the lights died on the phone. All contact with the outside world was lost. Steve sat on one side of the raft and Q on the other, eyes wide like saucers. Calmly Q asked Steve, "Are we going to die now?" Steve mulled the question over. "No," he said, "their job is to find us; our job is to stay alive."

Stranded in the Southern Ocean, 30 miles off the coast of Antarctica, the two men needed all the strength and collective will they could muster to survive, but all would have been without hope in the absence of satellite technology. A satellite phone enabled Steve to convey news of their whereabouts to Joanna, and in addition, their emergency beacon had been transmitting a distress signal from the moment they had ditched in the ocean.

"My mobile rang," says Joanna - this in the middle of the night - "it was RAF Kinloss, Scotland, ringing to confirm whether or not the distress signal they had received was from Steve, whether I had heard anything." So the EPIRB had done its job; Joanna was in a position to inject urgency to the search and rescue by confirming to RAF Kinloss that, yes, against the odds, the two men were indeed alive. In another most unlikely coincidence, Joanna also had an old school friend staying with her

who was married to a former Chilean Naval pilot, Seb Sheppard. The couple had never stayed with Joanna before; nor since. But that night Seb was at hand phoning old friends in Santiago and Antarctica, injecting further emotional energy into the rescue effort.

Meanwhile, Steve and Q were adjusting to the precarious position in which they found themselves, afloat a very large and cold expanse of sea in a very small 1960s liferaft. It didn't pass their notice that they were lucky to have a liferaft at all. At Heathrow, en route to Punta Arenas, they had come perilously close to abandoning it when flight officials suspected its compressed air cylinder (essential to inflate the craft) might be a bomb. Q explained that the dinghy was aviation-safe - indeed, that it had been designed especially to carry in helicopters and planes - but that if the authorities deemed they couldn't take it, then of course they wouldn't take it, that was fine, hopefully they wouldn't need it anyway. "Though", he added, "if we ditch in the Southern Ocean, on your head be it!" "OK mate," said the amiable official, "you take it."

Another wave crashed over the side of the dinghy, filling it with water. Steve found a small bag in the dinghy, containing six metal poles and a length of material. He slotted the poles into six pockets around the edge of the dinghy and stretched the length of the material over them, "like a child's sheet with elastic corners", to create a roof.

"Still," he says, "every five minutes or so, a large wave would approach and we'd lie broadside to balance the liferaft and stop it flipping, but freezing sea water would burst through between the main body of the raft and the roof filling it once more."

Steve and Q knew that like an ice bucket it would be the water that would kill them not the cold air. So armed with a plastic bag and a thermos, they worked hour after hour at bailing the freezing Antarctic

waters from their tiny raft. The little liferaft had been tightly packed, in reserve, in wait for such an eventuality as this, for 30 years.

"Sitting in it," says Q, "I had swirls of brown and purple imagery dancing in my head; and then I remembered: the swirls were those of the 1970s carpet in our home when I was a kid." Q recalls this unlikely association with some emotion. "I remember Dad assembling all the survival kit on the sitting room carpet: tins of fresh water, desalination kit, fishing hooks, patches to fix the dinghy, a mirror and a knife - all with huge care and the experience offered him as a naval commander."

So the little liferaft was almost as old as Q himself but, he argues, it was the very old-fashioned flimsiness of it that kept them alive. Complacency in such conditions might have been the kiss of death; but in the leaky dinghy they were continuously employed, bailing out the water!

The two men were gainfully employed ridding water from inside their survival suits as well. They were good survival suits, designed by Helly Hansen for operators on the North Sea oil rigs, but both men had been wearing them with the fixed hood down to accommodate head sets, and as a result, the necks of the suits were unsealed when they jumped into the sea.

"We had to take it in turns to unzip our suits and balance on our elbows while the other person lifted our legs and drained out as much water as possible," explains Steve, "then squeeze water down the sleeves and through the wrist straps." The extreme cold was going to be a serious problem. The air was 2°C and the water only just above freezing point. A few hours passed and Q lost movement in his legs; a short while later and Steve's legs too were out of action. At one point Q complained he was hot and started taking off his hood

and gloves. "We had a bit of a row about it," explains Steve, "he felt he was just hot and I felt it was the first stages of hypothermia. I literally had to punch him to see sense and keep his clothes on."

Their chances of survival were slipping away. "I knew we had to keep positive," says Steve. "Joanna had sent me a fax just before we left saying, good luck on the Drake Passage and keep an eye out for the Wandering Albatross. And right from the moment we crashed a huge albatross, one of the largest, most magnificent birds in the world, picked up our liferaft and flew overhead for the duration of our trial. These are wonderful birds that can sleep on the wing and stay at sea for up to three weeks at a time. It gave me great strength; made me feel quite sure Joanna was there with us and that everything was fine at home. We just had to stay alive."

They had been in the liferaft six, maybe seven hours, when at last they heard what they had been hoping beyond hope to hear: an aeroplane flying overhead. It was flying in a search pattern; they could hear it repeatedly coming closer and then fading away, and Steve loaded a flare gun. The plane did another pass. They still couldn't see it through the clouds and not wanting to waste their one flare, Steve decided to wait, until it did another pass. But, to his astonishment, it didn't do another pass. Instead, it flew away.

"That was a low moment," confesses Steve, one that might easily have led to despair. But Steve consciously, deliberately, turned his mind around. "I sat on the edge of the raft looking up at the sky," he says. "Repeatedly I said to the pilot, somewhere out there: 'There's no rush but you're going to come back right over this liferaft.' It was total positive thought. You ARE going to come back."

Their situation was desperate, their bodies slowly shutting down in their war of attrition against the cold. And yet the sea was pleasantly calm

by this stage, and the albatross still flying overhead. Steve speaks of the staggering beauty before his eyes and of his feelings, far from hopeless. And sure enough, 40 minutes later, the aeroplane - a little red Twin Otter from the Chilean Air Force - appeared as if from nowhere.

Steve grabbed the flare gun. His hands were frozen, infuriatingly ineffective. At last, he cocked the trigger. The plane was directly overhead almost too late to see the shot. He fired it and it blasted a scarlet flame, alarmingly close to the plane's cockpit, just to the fore of one of the engines on the wing.

Steve had the privilege to talk to the pilot, Captain Serda, at a later date. He had apparently been searching for them for a good couple of hours and was on the point of giving up, when he saw a red flash. He thought one of his engines was ablaze! And was about to shut one of the engines down, except that his instruments suggested the temperature and pressure of each was fine. Instead he turned the plane around for one last look, and there, through a thin veil of cloud, was a very, very small liferaft - a mere pinprick in a vast expanse of sea.

Soon Steve and Q were treated to the blast of a ship's fog horn - "the most warming of sounds," says Steve - and through the haze loomed the Chilean ice-breaker, Almirante Viel. Two frogmen were lowered into the water. They pulled the raft alongside the ship. A sling was lowered and Q lifted aboard, immediately to lose consciousness. Steve, confident that his lower body, though numb, still maintained its strength, attempted to climb the ship's netting onboard, and collapsed, his legs buckling beneath him. But the two men were at last in safe hands. Ten hours afloat a tiny 1960s liferaft, and they'd survived.

The collective emotion was one of relief. The two pilots were spoiled and pampered aboard the

boat: Q was dumped in a hot bath and massaged by the crew for a good half an hour; both men were issued crisp, cotton clothes and bunk beds with clean sheets. They slept soundly for hours and were later invited to join the captain for a celebration in the officers' mess.

Back at home, Joanna had remained cool and stoic throughout, handling calls from anxious brothers and mothers and enquiring reporters alike, ever calm, ever trusting of her husband's spirit to see him through, until, the news of their safety finally through, she took herself off to St George's Hospital, Tooting, for her first scan - yes, she was pregnant with their first child - and burst into tears.

For Joanna, for their unborn child, for himself, Steve was extraordinarily joyful to be alive, and grateful to those who had played such an active role in his and Q's rescue. As Q so aptly put it, their lives had been hanging "as if on a lady's cheap necklace". Yet, such is the nature of the wilful beast, that Steve, despite his joy and despite his indisputable gratitude, couldn't help but feel crucified as he watched the coast of Antarctica - the goal he had wanted for so long, and flown literally within minutes of attaining - slip away.

The day after their rescue, Steve and Q were transferred to the British ship, HMS Endurance and sailed for the Falkland Islands for their trip back to the U.K. "I thought with time it would become clear why we had crashed," says Steve, "whereas in fact it hasn't become clear at all. There was a catastrophic engine failure - we know that, but we've no idea why." This Steve seemed able to mentally package away, as a mystery beyond his powers to fathom. But his growing frustration at their failure, he could not. "Maybe we shouldn't have done it?" he found himself asking. Nobody passed judgement, but Steve sensed, or perhaps simply

projected upon himself, a collective, finger-pointing "told you so", an unspoken satisfaction that his ambition had been proven too bold.

"I was rocked by the failure," he says. From a place of optimism, he plunged into despair, until, a year or so on, the fear of misjudgement eventually eroded like soft shale around a granite core, and he rediscovered his resolve. Once more, he was able to voice with confidence, "we can do this".

In the midst of this emotional turnaround, though, life at Steve's and Joanna's London home had been turned on its head. On August 6th, 2003, their son, Jago, was born. Naturally, the new parents' attitude to life, adventure and risk shifted seismically - though to a different level on Joanna's Richter scale from Steve's.

"I never would have made that journey through the Americas with a child," says Joanna, "to this day I feel uncomfortable flying with Steve, leaving the kids at home." Steve, by contrast, fully recognised a responsibility to limit risk as far as it was feasibly possible, but not to limit that which he had full intent to do.

"I realised metaphorically I couldn't cycle without a helmet anymore," says Steve. "And I realised, too, I'd have to give up my old ways. I was stubbornly independent, arrogant the first time around, resisting the need to get a permit, that sort of thing. But I came to realise that none of us is an island; nothing of any scale can be done alone. If Q and I were to give it another go and succeed, we had to collaborate and work with others."

Steve set to work: winning approval from the Americans and Argentineans (to return to the Chileans, he recognised as a step too far); organising search and rescue; sorting fuel logistics; and splashing out on a new, bumble-bee black and yellow R44 Raven 2, with

"Their flight was a fleeting visit to an enchanting heaven on Earth made up of exquisite shades of turquoise and white."

fuel injection to boost performance at altitude and a modified fuel tank to increase the helicopter's range. Also on the shopping list was a spanking new liferaft (just in case) and fluorescent yellow survival suits that sealed around the neck! Every 'i' was dotted and 't' crossed. Never, quite, would Steve win the full approval of his wife; but Joanna understood, as did Steve, that it was imperative for him to give this project another crack if ever he was to move forward in life. He needed to prove to himself and to others that it was indeed possible to fly a small single-engine helicopter across the Drake Passage and on to the South Pole. "Failure," says Steve with passion, "isn't falling down; it's not getting up again."

Christmas 2004 and Steve, with Q, flew to Argentina for their second attempt to fly the 600 miles of open water to Antarctica while Joanna took 18-month-old Jago in her arms and flew to Sydney, to join her sister and some friends. "I wasn't going to sit at home waiting by the phone again," she says.

Come January 10th, 2005, and the weather forecast on the Drake Passage was good, and Steve and Q once again lifted a small R44 helicopter into the sky, direction south. Four-and-a-half hours of clear skies is what they needed - nothing more.

Half-an-hour into the flight and everything was running just as planned, and the pilots' spirits were high. The weather though, ever fickle, is particularly so in the Drake Passage, and ahead of them they could see an unexpected band of cloud. The two pilots registered concern but made a decision at this point to trust in their weather forecast, and flew on. 180 miles out into the Drake Passage, they reached the band of cloud and dropped altitude to fly beneath it. The outside temperature was 5°C and the visibility far from good. They flew another 20 miles, the temperature continuing to fall - gradually at first, then dramatically.

"The air temperature is -0.5°C," said Steve. "That's a shame," replied Q. The cold front took them completely by surprise. "It absolutely wasn't forecast," says Steve. The two pilots had a weather check in real time; they knew the weather conditions on the other side of the front were good, if only they could get there.

For the moment they were flying in freezing fog. The visibility was poor - cloud down to the sea - but of far greater concern was the imminent danger of ice building up on the machine. If the rotor blades took on too much ice, they would cease to be aerodynamic and stop working; and the last thing the two men wanted was to ditch for a second time in the Southern Ocean.

"We were watching water droplets on the skids and could just see them starting to form ice. It was pretty nerve-wracking," says Steve. "The question was just how much further we'd have to push to get through the front; we couldn't afford for it to get any colder." "By this time we were past the point of no return," adds Q. They no longer had enough fuel to fly back to South America. The only way forward was south to Antarctica.

In the end the two men stuck with it. At this point they had little choice - and good fortune flew with them. The little helicopter made it through the cold front and out the other side; the cloud lifted and the temperature rose just enough to prevent any further freezing.

And then there before them - for a second time - was a clear and magnificent view of Antarctica. They brought down the little helicopter to land at the Argentinean Jubany base at the southern tip of King George Island, the strain of the flight all too apparent in the deepened furrows on their brows, and the nervous overflow of their indubitable joy.

It might have been tempting for them to think at this point, the

Drake Passage successfully crossed, that they were on the home straight, that the South Pole was in the bag. But Steve and Q had to keep their wits about them for a further 2,500 miles yet.

After enjoying generous hospitality at the Argentinian research station at Jubany Base, they flew south and west, taking in views of the spectacular, not to mention historical landmarks of Greenwich, Half Moon, Livingston and Snow Islands, known to sealers from the early years of the 19th century.

Beneath them also they saw Deception Island - volcanic, almost circular in form - with a vast caldera flooded by the sea that's long provided ships refuge from Antarctic storms. Once again, they caught sight of Smith Island, where Steve and Q had made their own history, ditching their helicopter 35 miles off its northern coast. From here they swung south south west over 80 miles of open water to the Ukrainian base, Vernandsky, on the west coast of the Antarctic Peninsula.

At Vernandsky there was a very real danger their Pole to Pole expedition might be side-tracked by the warmth of Slavic hospitality and finished off completely with an overdose of home-brewed vodka – so much so that Steve and Q made the conscious decision to flee their new-found friends and pitch camp with the penguins instead, until the weather cleared and they were able to continue their southbound journey to Alexander Island. Here, Steve and Q met their supply team who had flown across from Patriot Hills.

Patriot Hills is an area of naturally occurring blue ice - inland on mainland Antarctica, at an altitude of some 3,000ft - that has acted as a perfect runway for large jets and subsequently been home to a semi-permanent logistics support camp for various Antarctic expeditions for some 30 years. Based here was

Mike Sharp, director of Antarctic Logistics & Expeditions (ALE), who was providing fuel for Steve and Q on the continent, as well as search and rescue.

"The supply team had three drums of Avgas on board, and my dear friend and film-maker, Sean Davidson," says Steve. "His enthusiasm at being in such an incredible place was infectious and lifted our spirits which had been so focussed on the job in hand."

Their flight, south along the western coast of Antarctica, turned out to be a fleeting visit to an enchanting heaven on Earth made up of exquisite shades of turquoise and white. Beneath them stretched a jigsaw puzzle of gleaming pack ice on ink black

pre-designated point on the ice. As Steve and Q made their way towards it, they flew under cloud, and the visibility took a decided turn for the worse.

"When you have cloud above and snow below, everything turns white. It's a very dangerous situation," says Steve. "You become unable to judge if you are 20 feet or 200 feet above the ground."

And it's no use relying on instruments in such conditions. A radar altimeter transmits a sonic beep and measures the time it takes to bounce back from the ground, and from this calculates the distance - like a bat. But if the ground over which the helicopter is flying is snow, the sonic beep is partially absorbed, and the reading erratic.

face to the next, black in a scene that was otherwise white, and flew from one visual cue to another. Finally, they spotted the small cluster of fuel barrels that had been left waiting for them by ALE, and using these as visual references in the white, were able to land. After another half-an-hour, the cloud lifted, and they flew the last 300 miles to Patriot Hills.

From here, it was just one fuel dump and 600 miles to the South Pole - plus a gradual ascent of 7,000ft up and up the glacial dome of the Antarctic ice cap that reaches its greatest thickness, and height, at an altitude of nearly 10,000ft. It's as well the R44 Raven 2 engine was fitted with fuel injection.

There was just one major topographical feature en route: the Thiele Mountains. Otherwise it was like an endless sea of ice. "An Antarctic heaven, extraordinarily pure," says Steve, just reward for a journey of 27,000 miles so nearly completed. Two years after their setting off from the North Pole at the very top of the world, and after all his flying adventures with Joanna, Steve and Q were within striking distance of landing at the South Pole at the very bottom of the world.

Until, within just five miles of their goal, an incident of indefinable nature threatened to stop them in their tracks.

The South Pole, unlike that in the North, is home to an American scientific base, named after the man who first reached this most southerly spot on Earth, and his rival who sacrificed his life in his attempt to do so: the Amundsen-Scott South Pole Station. And on the day Steve and Q chose to land there, it was closed.

"It was the most extraordinary situation," says Steve. "They told us they were too busy to talk to us on the radio, and asked us not to land at the South Pole but to land five

miles short and camp, and review the situation the following day." Not entirely surprisingly, Steve and Q decided to risk the American's wrath and flew above the control zone over the Pole - just to cover all eventualities - before retreating to a safe distance and pitching camp. Their fear was that if they shut down the helicopter's engine at 10,000ft and 30 degrees below zero, it might not start again. And come morning, their fear was realised. Only extraordinary ingenuity and the building of an igloo around the helicopter's base to encase a liquid gas burner and warm the engine compartment, enabled them to start the engine and head back to the South Pole, this time to land.

The sense of achievement as, at last, they touched the Raven's skids on the ice was intense. They had tried once, and failed - very nearly lost their lives, and picked themselves up and tried again. "Not only was it the most beautiful trip," says Q, "but the unloading of a huge burden, an intense, life-time high."

For Steve, it was also an entry into the record books, the first person to fly a helicopter from Pole to Pole. "Such a privilege," he says, "to fly around our planet from tip to toe, at 200ft above the ground, sometimes 10ft above the ground, to witness its animals, and peoples, and ever changing landscapes, in all its majesty. We can indeed do anything to which we set our minds, belief wins in the end," he says.

"But only when we acknowledge the help of others. The team is everything. I understand that at a far deeper level at the completion of this expedition than I did at the start. Without a change of attitude within, without Q, without Joanna - that wonderful journey we did together - without everyone who put their all into the planning and logistics, it would have remained only a fanciful idea hatched over a glass of wine around the kitchen table."

"When you have cloud above and snow below, everything turns white. It's a very dangerous situation," says Steve. "You become unable to judge if you are 20ft or 200ft above the ground."

water; icebergs, broken free of the continental ice cap, upturned like giant molars and captured again in a frozen sea; a crazy geometry of windblown, sculptured snow atop glacial ice sliced with crevasses; and translucent blue green lakes with floating water lilies of ice, sprinkled with sparkling crystals around the edges like cocktail glasses with salt. "We'd worked hard to get here," says Steve, "but the reward was unbelievable."

Before long, though, they were to witness a more treacherous side of Antarctica. From the coast, they were to fly inland to Patriot Hills, touching down just once to pick up some fuel that Mike Sharp and his team had dropped at a

At the fore of Steve's and Q's mind was also a horrendous incident that had occurred in similar conditions just one year before. Pilots Jennifer Murray and Colin Bodill, also attempting to be the first to fly from Pole to Pole, crashed in whiteout conditions on the Ronne Ice Shelf in Antarctica. Both pilots sustained serious injuries but managed to hastily erect a tent and sit it out in sub-zero temperatures until ALE flew a team of medics to the rescue. The simple rule, even for the most experienced of Antarctic pilots, is not to fly if there is any risk of a white out.

Steve's and Q's visibility was dangerously limited, but they picked their way from one rock

South Pole Station

ANTARCTICA - LAND OF HEROES

Antarctica is the coldest place on Earth. It is also the windiest, the driest and one of the most pure and beautiful, especially in the summer months when the sun hovers above the horizon from one long day to the next.

Belief in the existence of a Terra Australis - a vast continent in the far south of the globe - existed since Ptolemy suggested the idea as a balance to the northern lands of Europe, Asia and North Africa, in the 1st century AD. But it remained illusive for centuries. The first sighting of the continent was as recently as 1820, by a Russian expedition led by Mikhail Lazarey and Fabian Gottlieb von Bellingshausen. It was the last discovered continent in the world.

Even so, it remained largely neglected for much of the 19th century because of the hostility of its environment and isolation. It wasn't until the establishment figures of the International Geographical Congress in London opined that "the exploration of the Antarctic Regions is the greatest piece of geographical exploration still to be undertaken," in 1985, that the curtains were opened on the 'Heroic Age of Antarctic Exploration'.

Australian Douglas Mawson was one of the four pre-eminent names of this era. A geologist on the British Antarctic Expedition of 1907, he went on to be a member of the first team to reach the South Magnetic Pole, assuming leadership on their perilous return when one of their number plus dogs and sledge fell into a crevasse and were lost. It was a Norwegian team, led by explorer Roald Amundsen, who first set foot on the geographic South Pole on December 14th, 1911, only a narrow margin of days before the ill-fated British expedition led by Robert Falcon Scott.

And then there was the epic Ernest Shackleton expedition of 1914-16 which aimed to cross Antarctica from sea to sea and failed before even reaching land. Shackleton's ship Endurance was beset in the ice, crushed and sunk. But the story of Shackleton's undaunted courage, leading all his men to safety, is one that thrills readers to this day. "For scientific discovery give me Scott," said Sir Edmund Hillary, who himself reached the South Pole as part of the Commonwealth Trans-Antarctic Expedition, in 1958, "for speed and efficiency of travel give me Amundsen; but when disaster strikes and all hope is gone, get down on your knees and pray for Shackleton."

Much has been learned about the icy continent since the days of the early explorers. It is a desert, with precipitation of only 8 inches a year along the coast and far less inland. It has the highest average elevation of all the continents. Some 98 per cent of the continent is covered in ice, much of it over one mile thick. It holds about 70 per cent of the world's fresh water, and if it were to melt, sea levels would rise by about 200ft.

Antarctica has no government and belongs to no country. The Antarctic Treaty, signed in 1959 by twelve countries and a further thirty-four since, prohibits military activities and mineral mining, supports scientific research and protects the continent's environment. To this day there are no permanent human residents on the continent. Just 5,000 or so temporary residents of government-maintained scientific research station dotted around the continent - a number which dwindles closer to a 1,000 in the winter months. Plus an increasing number of tourists, most who visit by boat to view Antarctica's striking coastline and wealth of marine wildlife, and a miniscule number who - like Steve and Q - venture into the interior.

"For scientific discovery give me Scott," said Sir Edmund Hillary, "for speed and efficiency of travel give me Amundsen; but when disaster strikes and all hope is gone, get down on your knees and pray for Shackleton."

PICTURE CREDITS

p7: Going north from Ward Hunt Island, Canada.

p8: Nissen Hut, Ward Hunt Island, Canada.

p9-10: The mountains of Ellesmere Island, Canada.

p11-12: Ice at Mould Bay, Canada

p13: Open water lead, 60 miles from the North Pole.

p14: A real Fox's Glacier Mints polar bear shot.

p15: Steve elatedly circling G-NUDE parked on top of the world
– the North Pole.

p16: Q with controls, Northwest passage, Canada.

p24: Chugach Mountains, Alaska.

p25: Pools of blue glacial melt water, Tazlina Glacier,
Chugach Mountains, Alaska.

p26: An Alaskan bald eagle soaking up the sun, Yakutat Bay, Alaska.

p27: A harbor seal colony near Mt. Fairweather, Alaska.

p28: Low level coastal flight near Cross Sound, Alaska.

p29: The pristine wilderness with snow, forests and sea, Alaska.

p30: A self-fashioned floatplane launch, Cordova, Alaska.

p31: Archipelago in the Queen Charlotte Sound, British Columbia, Canada.

p34: Our campsite on a small island, known to us as 'Big Bear Island,' Canada.

p35: Downtown Vancouver, Canada.

p36: Hauling lumber the Canadian way down the
Queen Charlotte Strait, Canada.

p37: The turquoise glacial melt meeting the tree line, near Bella Bella, Canada.

p39: A sea fret rolling over the hills of Washington, USA.

p42: Customs officers at Bellingham International Airport, Washington, USA.

p43: Fog clinging to the hilltops just north of Sacramento, California, USA.

p45: Crossing the foothills into the Sierra Nevada, California, USA.

p48: Our campsite on a cattle ranch just outside the Mojave Desert, USA.

p49: Burt Rhutan's sub-orbital space plane Spaceship One,
Mojave Desert, USA.

p51: Circles of irrigated land in the desert, Arizona, USA.

p54: Following the 'Road to Nowhere,' Arizona, USA.

p55: Vast canyons north of Prescott, Arizona, USA.

p57: Afternoon storm cells building, New Mexico, USA.

p60: Vast canyons north of Prescott, Arizona, USA.

p61: Almost like a wave - Gypsum Sand at the White Sands National
Monument, Alamogordo, New Mexico, USA.

p63: Flying into the main terminal in San Antonio Airport, Houston,
Texas, USA.

p66: The vast fertile plains of Texas, USA.

p67: Wind farms, West Texas. Courtesy of Aerial Archives/Alamy.

p71: Flying south towards Mexico near Padre Island, Texas, USA.

p74: Fertile hillsides just south of Veracruz, Mexico.

p75: Laguna Madre, Mexico.

p76: Our swimming spot at Ciudad del Carmen, Mexico.

p77: The ancient Mayan ruins at Chichen Itza, Mexico.

p79: Low level coastal flight north of the Cayes, Belize.

p82: The highlands of Belize on the Guatemalan border.

p83: Caye Caulker, Belize.

p85: Traditionally dressed women in Solola, Guatemala.

p88: Fertile land on the edge of Lake Atitlan, Guatemala.

p89: Older traditionally dressed woman, Solola, Guatemala.

p90: Crowds at the celebration.

p91: The ancient Mayan ruins of Tikal, Guatemala.

p93: Marshalling alongside international carriers. Where?

p96: Incredibly dense rainforests of Honduras.

p97: Cloud forests, Honduras.

p99: San Cristobal Volcano, the highest volcano in Nicaragua
at 5725 ft, Nicaragua.

p102: Street scenes in Granada, Nicaragua.

p103: Schoolgirl in the colonial streets of Granada, Nicaragua.

p105: G-Nude surfing the Pacific coast of Costa Rica.

p108: Entering Costa Rica, just south of La Cruz.

p109: Sets of waves, Pacific surf, Costa Rica.

p111: Panama City, Panama.

p114: Isla Boca islands, off the east coast of Panama.

p115: Traditionally dressed Kuna woman, San Blas islands, Panama.

p116: Two fishermen chat beside the helicopter, San Blas islands, Panama.

p117: Traditionally adorned women, San Blas islands, Panama.

p118: Traditionally adorned women, San Blas islands, Panama.

p119: Traditionally adorned women, San Blas islands, Panama.

p123: Roof tops, Cartegena. Courtesy of Seb Agudelo/Alamy.

p124: Yellow buildings, Cartagena. Courtesy of Glow Images/Alamy.

p126: Coloured buildings, Cartagena – Colombia.

p127: The Darien Gap, Colombia.

p128: Kogi Indian Huts, Colombia. Courtesy of Brian Latino/Alamy.

p129: Auyan Tepui in the Lost World, Venezuela.

p132: Houses on stilts, Lake Maracaibo, Venezuela.

p133: Dense forest along the banks of a tributary,
Canaima National Park, Venezuela.

p135: Waterfalls in Canaima National Park, Venezuela.

p136: Angel Falls, Canaima National Park, Venezuela.

p137: A classic oxbow river of the Amazon, Brazil.

p140: The confluence of rivers Negro and Solimoes at the point
where the Amazon is formed, Manaus, Brazil.

p141: Flying low along the banks of the Amazon, Brazil.

p142: Vein-like tributaries of the Amazon, Brazil.

p143: An impression of the sheer scale of the Amazon rainforest, Brazil.

p145: A lone fisherman at sunset, the Amazon, Peru.

p148: Traditional woman with goat, market town, Sacred Valley Peru.

p149: Villagers from the outskirts of Iquitos, Peru.

p150: Children on the outskirts of Iquitos, Peru.

p151: Machu Picchu, Peru. Courtesy of Micah Hanson/Alamy.

p153: Tango dancers, Señor Tango, Buenos Aires, Argentina.

p156: Vast open horizons just outside Neuquén, Argentina.

p157: Flamingos, Tierra del Fuego, Argentina.

p158: Mud flats, Tierra del Fuego, Argentina.

p159: Perito Moreno Glacier, El Calafate, Patagonia, Argentina.

p160: Lunar landscape, Tierra del Fuego, Argentina.

p161: The twisted flag trees of Patagonia, Argentina.

p162: The runway at Rio Gallegos, Argentina.

p163: Cattle ranching with the Gauchos, Salta, Argentina.

p165: A pass leading to the Almirantazgo Fjord, Chile.

p168: An estancia in Tierra del Fuego, Argentina.

p169: The Drake Passage, Atlantic and Pacific Oceans.

p176: Entering the George VI Sound, Antarctica.

p177: Le Maire Strait, Antarctica.

p178: Flying through natural ice sculptures near Graham Island, Antarctica.

p179: Q parked on a towering iceberg near Adelaide Island, Antarctica.

p180: Iceberg graveyard, Marguerite Bay, Antarctica.

p181: Our shadow, Antarctica.

p182: The stillness of ice at dusk, Antarctica.

p184: Camps at Patriot Hills, antarctica

p185: Camp at 10,000 feet, 5 miles from the South Pole, Antarctica.

p186: Thiel Mountains, Antarctica.

p187: Iceberg graveyard, Marguerite Bay, Antarctica.

p188: They made it; the boys at the south pole.

p189: South Pole station, Antarctica